AN ICONOGRAPHER'S SKETCHBOOK:

DRAWINGS & PATTERNS

VOLUME II, THE TYULIN COLLECTION

Translations & Commentary by
GREGORY MELNICK

OAKWOOD PUBLICATIONS
1998

AN ICONOGRAPHER'S SKETCHBOOK:
DRAWINGS & PATTERNS
VOLUME II, THE TYULIN COLLECTION

Translations & Commentary by
GREGORY MELNICK

OAKWOOD PUBLICATIONS

© 1998 OAKWOOD PUBLICATIONS
3827 Bluff Street
Torrance California 90505
Telephone: (310) 378-9245

Published by Philip Tamoush

Cover by Copyright Graphics, Lomita, California

ISBN: 1-879038-22-6

The Sketches were published originally as **Образцы Древнерусской Иконописи. Пере-воды изъ собранія М. В. Тюлина. М И. и В. И. Успенскіе. Издано при С. Петербургскомъ Археологическомъ Институтѣ. С. П. Б. 1899.** Patterns of Old Russian Iconography from the Collection of M. V. Tyulin. M[ichael] I[vanovich] and V[asili]. I[vanovich]. Uspensky, Published by the St. Petersburg Archaeological Institute, St. Petersburg, 1899. And **Матеріалы для Исторіи Русскаго Иконописанія. Переводы изъ Собранія И. Б. Тюлина. М. И. и В. И. Успенскіе. Издано при С. Петер-бугскомъ Археологическомъ Институтѣ. С. П. Б. 1900.** Materials for the History of Russian Iconography from the Collection of I. V. Tyulin. M[ichael] I[vanovich] and V[asili]. I[vanovich]. Uspensky, Published by the St. Petersburg Archaeological Institute, St. Petersburg, 1900.

TABLE OF CONTENTS

**96 Sketches from
"Patterns of Old Russian Iconography
From the Collection of M. V. Tyulin," 1899**

**101 Sketches from
"Materials for the History of Russian Iconography
from the Collection of I. V. Tyulin," 1900**

INTRODUCTION

THE SECOND volume of the Iconographers's Sketchbook assumes familiarity with the first volume. It seemed better to present two articles of which the reader might not be aware rather than reprint material from the first volume. For the information and edification of iconographers I have selected two articles which express balanced approaches to traditional iconography.

Archbishop John (Maximovich) was a spiritual phenomenon. Those who knew him have described him as a living source of God's wonders, the embodiment of all Christian virtues, a miracle of ascetic firmness, a model archpastor, who had the gift of being able to see into the human heart and bring it to Christ. His sermon "Concerning Talents and Iconography" is reprinted here with the gracious permission of the Nicodemus Orthodox Publication Society from *Man of God: Saint John of Shanghai & San Francisco*.

Helena Kontzevich saw almost a century of Orthodoxy both in Russia and in the West. With her outstanding scholarship she combined a spiritual sobriety bequeathed by her ties to the last Optina Elders and her staunch traditionalism. Her husband was the renowned Russian theologian, Professor Ivan M. Kontzevich, brother of the blessed Bishop Nectary of Seattle. Her uncle Serge Nilus discovered the manuscript of Motovilov's famous conversation with St. Seraphim of Sarov. Her article "Russian Icons from an Ecclesio-historical Perspective" is reprinted here in its entirety with the kind permission of the fathers of St. Gregory Palamas Monastery.

Father Steven Bigham has written a book about God the Father in art which returns us to the roots of Orthodox iconography from which practitioners have strayed so completely, especially in recent centuries. A few selections from his "Canons on Iconography" are presented in the Appendix for convenient reference.

I would like to thank A. Charles Kovacs for reducing the drawings to a manageable size and Karyl Knee for searching for missing drawings. Most of all, I would like to thank Philip Tamoush for encouraging me by his dedication to Orthodox iconography.

Having painted icons since 1961 when there were so few pictures of icons available, and knowing how difficult it is to design "original" icons, I sincerely hope this new edition of the Postnikov and Tyulin Collections* will be an inspiration to my fellow icon painters and aid the painting of modern traditional Orthodox icons.

Gregory Melnick
Syracuse, New York
May, 1998.

---

* *An Iconographer's Sketchbook Volume I* contains the two volumes of the Postnikov Collections. *An Iconographer's Sketchbook Volume II* contains the two volumes of the Tyulin Collections, published separately.

CONCERNING TALENTS AND ICONOGRAPHY

By Saint John of Shanghai & San Francisco

THE LORD SPOKE a parable about a master who distributed talents to his servants, each man according to his abilities. After a certain time had passed, he demanded an accounting from each and rewarded those who earned as much as they had received. But the one who did nothing and simply returned the talent he had been given was punished severely. The master is the Lord God, the talents are His gifts, the servants are men. The Lord grants spiritual gifts; He grants them to individuals, and also to entire nations.

Until the Coming of Christ, God's words were entrusted to Israel. When Israel wavered in faith, when Judea began to fall, the Prophet Baruch, a disciple of the Prophet Jeremiah, called out, *This is the book of the commandments of God, and the law that endureth for ever: all they that keep it shall come to life; but such as leave it shall die. Turn thee, O Jacob, and take hold of it: walk of the light thereof, that thou mayest be illuminated. Give not thine honor to another, nor the things that are profitable unto thee to a strange nation. O Israel, happy are we; for things that are pleasing to God are made known unto us.*[*]

Israel, however, did not keep God's commandments, rejecting the Son of God, fell away from God. The Lord founded His New Testament Church, into which many formerly pagan peoples entered. After Christianity's victory over paganism, Byzantium became the special guardian of Orthodoxy. There the Ecumenical Councils and Holy Fathers of the Church established a precise exposition of the dogmas of the Faith and Orthodox teaching. After the fall of Byzantium, the Orthodox Faith was preserved best by the Russian people, who by that time had thoroughly absorbed it. Their way of life, the country's civil laws, its customs—all were grounded in the Orthodox faith or conformed to it.

One representation of the Orthodox Faith is the temple, and the Russian land was covered with them. The Orthodox temple itself is an image of the invisible universal Church, of which we speak in the Symbol of Faith: "In One Holy, Catholic (meaning "universal")[**] and Apostolic Church." This is why our temples are also called churches. Rising aloft, the cupola symbolizes for us a striving towards Heaven and reminds us of the

---

[*] (Baruch 4:1-4)

[**] [When preaching in or translating from Russian one must point out that the Church Slavonic word for "catholic" in the Symbol of Faith is соборную. This adjective formed from the root word "sobor" may cause confusion because it sounds like it means "conciliar" or "of the councils."]

heavenly vaults beneath which our prayers ascend to God. It reminds us of the invisible heavens, God's kingdom on high.

Churches are adorned with icons. Icons are not simply pictures of certain people or events. An icon is a symbol of the invisible. It depicts not only the outward, visible countenance of the Lord and His saints, but also their inner likeness, their sanctity. Even secular paintings often personify certain ideas. Let us take, for example, the famous statue of Peter the Great in Petrograd; here he is represented high up on a rearing horse, symbolic of how high, in many respects, he raised up Russia. Many other statues similarly convey certain ideas. If this is true of secular art, it should be true all the more of religious art, which portrays the sublime, the heavenly, the spiritual. An icon is not a portrait; a portrait depicts only a person's earthly aspect, while an icon depicts also his inner state. Even if only the external features are depicted, at different times the subject will have a different expression. Blessed Metropolitan Anthony related how, as a student at the Theological Academy, he and some classmates attended services in Kronstadt celebrated by righteous Father John. When Father John ended the Liturgy he appeared radiant, just like Moses when he came down from Mount Sinai. Shortly afterwards Father John received them in his cell and was his usual self. Our Lord Jesus Christ Himself once showed us His divine glory on Mount Tabor, while at other times He looked like an ordinary man, and people wondered, amazed, at the source of His power and miracles.

An icon ought to depict not only the outward but also the inner life, holiness and closeness to heaven. This is depicted primarily in the face and its expression, and the rest of the icon should conform to this. Our Orthodox iconographers directed all their attention to conveying the state of the soul, concealed beneath the flesh. The more successful this attempt was, the better the icon was. The execution of other parts of the body was frequently inadequate, not because this was done consciously by the iconographers but because the attainment of their principal goal did not always allow them to pay sufficient attention to secondary aspects. One might add that even in taking ordinary photographs, especially candid ones, many would undoubtedly show unnatural positions of the body, which ordinarily we would not notice. One cannot paint an icon by depicting the external aspect alone; this external representation must reflect the unseen struggles and must radiate with heavenly glory. This can be achieved most successfully by the person who himself leads a spiritual life, and who understands and deeply reveres the lives of the saints. Our ancient iconographers, in engaging in this art, always prepared for it with prayer and fasting. To many icons executed in this manner the Lord granted wonder-working power.

Of course, every icon, after it is sanctified, should be revered and must not be treated with disdain or disrespect. We should therefore refrain from passing judgment on icons which have already found a place in churches, but we must always strive towards what is better, and, what is most important, our attention should be directed not so much towards the aesthetic appeal of icons as to their spirituality. Icons that do not satisfy the requirements of Orthodox iconography ought not be placed in churches or in homes. Icons cannot be painted by simply anyone who has a talent for art and who is capable of their artistic execution. Often the state of the person painting an icon and a desire to serve God are of greater significance than artistic skill. In Russia, after the reign of Peter the Great, along with the good which arrived from the West, many novelties foreign to the spirit of Orthodoxy entered into Russia. A significant portion of Russia's educated class fell under this influence, which injected much that was unhealthy and bad into their literary and artistic works. This tendency was also reflected in iconography. Instead of emulating the ancient Russian iconographers, they began to emulate artists of the West, who were unfamiliar with Orthodoxy. The new images, although they were very beautiful, did not correspond to the spirit of iconography. This spirit, foreign to Orthodoxy, began to take root in Russia and gradually unsettled her. The words of the prophet are addressed to us today: *Give not of thy glory to another, and what is beneficial to thee to an alien people.* Just as in life, so, too, in church traditions we must return to those firm and pure foundations on which Russia was built and secured herself. One reflection of these foundations is our iconography. Icons for our churches must not be painted in a spirit foreign to Orthodoxy. Some think this means icons must be painted in dark colors, with unnatural positioning of the bodies. This is not true. Ancient icons were painted with bright colors and darkened over time with the accumulation of dust. At the same time, it must be remembered that many saints were in fact dark-complexioned, having spent their lives in hot deserts, and many had bodies that were indeed emaciated with long years of ascetic struggle. Theirs was not an earthly but a heavenly beauty. Through their prayers may they help our churches become reflections of heavenly glory and help our flock to unite in seeking the Kingdom of God and to preach—not only through the church but also through life—the truth of Orthodoxy.*

---

* *Man of God,* pages 159 and following.

RUSSIAN ICONS FROM AN ECCLESIO-HISTORICAL PERSPECTIVE

by Helena Kontzevich

THE SUBJECT of iconography is not as simple as it might appear at first glance, and there exists a following of outstanding and world-renowned students devoted to the subject—not only among us (Russians), but in the West as well. The ancient Russian icon represents an extremely elaborate area of study and we cannot neglect that which has already been established in it. The goal of our article is to survey briefly the area from an ecclesio-historical perspective, in no way pretending, of course, to embrace thoroughly and completely such an expansive area of study in a brief article.

Orthodox icons appeared in Rus' from the time of her Baptism into Orthodoxy in 988. One of these ancient icons, the wonder-working "Vladimir" Mother of God, subsequently saved Moscow from a Tartar invasion. She was brought from Constantinople at the end of the eleventh, or at the beginning of the twelfth, century, and was first located in Vyshgorod near Kiev. In 1155 the icon was transferred to Vladimir by St. Andrew Bogolyubsky, and in 1395 was placed in Moscow's *Uspensky* (Dormition) Cathedral. At present it is located in the Tretiakov Gallery, after being cleaned of an exterior darkened layer.*

The visage of the Most-Holy Virgin is filled with an inexpressible, profound grief, apparently in anticipation of the future fulfillment of the prophecy of Symeon the God-Receiver. The Savior-Child tenderly comforts the grieving Mother of God. Another remarkable icon of the Theotokos, the "Great Panagia" or Oranta (end of the twelfth, or beginning of the thirteenth, century), was found in 1919 in the *Preobrazhensky* (Transfiguration) Monastery in Yaroslavl. Here the Theotokos is represented as a young virgin, standing at full-length with her arms expressing grief, and the God-Child is depicted as on the *Znameny* "Sign" Icon. On the sides are painted two angels with faces of indescribable beauty.

This article cannot contain the countless other remarkable icons of the pre-Mongol period.** At the time of the Tartar invasion, the blossoming of church art came to a halt. But in the fourteenth century there arose a *renaissance* of iconographic art throughout the entire Orthodox East, a stream of which flowed into the Russian lands also. Thus Charles Diehl, a member of the French Academy and professor at the Sarbonne, writes concerning this:

---

* [As this book was going to press, the May - June 1998 issue of *The Orthodox Church* reported that this icon was transferred to the Church of St. Nicholas in Tolmachi in Moscow on June 2 - publisher's note.]

** Tenth to thirteenth centuries -translator's note.

The art of Byzantium awoke for its last re-birth. This art lost its abstract character, becoming living and picturesque..., dramatic, captivating. Hued, harmonious, and skilled, its technique approached impressionism. Various schools were formed. One of these, in Constantinople, produced masterpieces with its mosaics; the masters of other schools beautified the churches in Macedonia, Old Serbia, and the ancient churches of Athos. In such a manner, Byzantium, outwardly exhausted, discovered in the fourteenth century, as earlier in the tenth, a new vibrant force in contact with ancient tradition; and with this powerful movement of art, similar to the revival in fourteenth-century Italy, with which, however, it possessed nothing in common, Byzantium expanded its influence in the entire eastern world: among Serbs, Russians, Romanians.

A wave of this fourteenth-century renewal (accurately portrayed by Professor Diehl, albeit in terms somewhat western and imprecise) swept from Serbia (Macedonia) to Rus', owing to uninterrupted intercourse between Russia and the East.* This glorious fourteenth century was made manifest in Rus' as a certain bright period of development, illuminating all areas of life. Then, for the first time, the Tartar Horde was defeated at the Battle of Kulikovo, 1380. Subsequently, disciples of St. Sergius of Radonezh established the beginnings of the growth of monastic colonization. About one hundred holy men, as heavenly lights, beautified this epoch with their sanctity.

This general ascendancy was reflected also in the church art of this time, and in iconography in particular was manifested in such figures as St. Andrei Rublev, Theophan the Greek, and others. These iconographers possessed an unparalleled faculty for harmonious combinations of colors and, most importantly, a faculty for capturing in the subjects portrayed in their icons and frescoes the marks of the highest spirituality, such as seen on the faces of saints. The art of the fourteenth and fifteenth centuries constituted a golden age of Russian iconography, never subsequently surpassed. But in 1453 the fall of Constantinople occurred, and soon the entire East fell under the yoke of the Turks. Meanwhile, in Italy the Renaissance began to reach fruition: an incarnation in art of the beauty of earthly life and the ancient pagan cult of the flesh, in marked contrast to an Orthodox iconography which manifests the expressions of the ascetic ideal and the revelation of the spiritual world and its beauty, the like of which is attained and manifested in the works of the great iconographers.

And thus, from the moment that the entire Orthodox East found itself under the power of the Turks, in Rus' the cultural influence of fellow-Orthodox countries ceased, this circumstance being further exacerbated by the perceived unfaithfulness of the

---

* Cf. I. Kontzevich, *The Acquisition of the Holy Spirit in the Ways of Ancient Russia*, Paris, 1952.

Orthodox Greeks, faith in whom had been undermined.* Russia at this time became locked-up within itself and, with the absence of educational centers, there arose a certain stagnation and decline in the spiritual life. Therefore, in 1551, in the better period of the reign of Ivan the Terrible, the 100-Chapters or Stoglav Council was convened.

The goal of the Stoglav Council was the renewal of the Russian Church and the correction of such inadequacies as had crept into the domain of church life. Its decrees touched on the divine services, the administration and proceedings of the episcopal eparchies, spiritual life, monasticism, and the religious life of the laity.

Among the resolutions of the Council were those pertaining to iconography. Certain "exemplars" were appointed, in conformity to Holy Tradition, to be used as models in the painting of icons. The icons selected were consistent with that handed down from the ancient past: icons which were spiritually inspired, possessing a sublime quality and evidencing passionlessness—since icons should be voiceless sermons and theology in image. These "exemplars" would allow even iconographers with mediocre skills to paint completely traditional icons adhering to the Holy Canons. The resolutions of the Stoglav Council were never rescinded by the Russian ecclesiastical authority. But what subsequently occurred in historical actuality?

As one contemporary historian has noted, "The reign of Ivan IV made manifest at the same time both the brilliant and the tragic, a reign in which were implanted the roots of the Petrine reforms and all the causes of the terrible catastrophe at the end of the sixteenth century," i.e., the "Time of Troubles." As a consequence of the invasion of the Polish armies deep within Russia, the first seeds of Western influence were sown. Indeed, the seventeenth century showed itself to be a century of decline. The confusion of the masses brought forth a change, and Russian life became bifurcated and confused, the wholeness of its world view having been lost. The past and its ethos "быть„ were shaken.

It was in the eighteenth century that a decisive break with the past finally took place. Peter I initiated an unconditional and blind process of imitating the West with his infamous reforms, and from this time forth the upper classes began to forget the great achievements of Russia's spiritual culture, traditions, and way of life. The goal of life became, not a preparation for Eternity and the acquisition of the Holy Spirit, but only that of material prosperity.

The Petrine reforms affected, above all else, church order. The patriarchate was transformed into a synod of bishops with a secular procurator at its head. Consequently,

---

* Mrs. Kontzevich refers to the fact that in Rus', during this time, the fall of Constantinople was often attributed to the betrayal of the Church by some of the Greek hierarchy and the emperor, who signed the infamous decrees of the pseudo-council of Florence. Hence the notion of Moscow as the "Third Rome" or inheritor of the status of Constantinople in the Orthodox world. In all fairness, it should be pointed out that the Metropolitan of Moscow also signed the infamous union decrees and became a cardinal in the Latin Church - translator's note.

the authority of the church was destroyed and her influence on Russian life undermined. The building of churches, iconography, and church singing succumbed to modernization along Western patterns, losing their previously great spiritual character and ethos. A complete retrogression occurred, as these elements of church life began to cater to the earthly tastes of a decadent epoch. The boundary between iconography and secular painting was erased. Thus it was that the artist Karl Briullov painted an icon of an angel with a censor and candle for a church in the Russian court, using for the visage of the angel a portrait of the deceased Grand Princess, the daughter of Emperor Nicholas I. He thus simply imitated Western artists, who often copied the figures in their religious paintings from living subjects.

Typifying this decline in iconography is Shmelov's short story, "The Unintoxicating Cup." It is also apropos of our own time, when cultured society has to a great extent lost an understanding of the spiritual. In this story, a robust artist, having studied in Italy, paints a portrait of his hostess, for whom he has a flaming secret passion, in the form of an icon of the Theotokos. This passion ultimately consumes him and he dies. Later, when the "icon"-portrait is found, it proves to be miracle-working. Here eroticism and emotion are blasphemously taken for spirituality!

Only at the beginning of the twentieth century, not long before World War I, when a universal reconsideration of values was undertaken in Russia, was the ancient icon recognized in the field of art as the greatest of artistic works. Unfortunately, this discovery, by reason of the shock attendant to it did not reach the consciousness of the believing masses. Let us note the words of a Russian student of icons, Professor (Prince) Eugene Trubetzskoi: "Until quite recently, icons were completely incomprehensible to the educated Russian. He hardly gave them a passing glance. He simply could not discern the icon under the age-old deposits of soot. Only in the very recent past have our eyes been opened to the uncommon beauty and vivid colors hidden beneath its soot. Only now, owing to the astonishing progress in contemporary techniques of restoration, can we behold these colors of past centuries, putting thus decisively to rest the myth that these icons were dark to begin with. It turns out that the darkened faces of the saints in our old churches were partly due to our inattention and neglect, partly due to our lack of skill in preserving these ancient treasures."

To these words we might add the observation that contemporary art, not iconographic art, fades; for, contemporary art expresses the tastes of its time. Thus, Karl Briullov and Brune embody, in the famous Church of Christ the Savior (which was destroyed by the Bolsheviks), the trends and style of the Nicholaevsky period and Basnetzov, in the Vladimir Cathedral, the aesthetic and decorative style of the time of Alexander III. We have already pointed out that only under Nicholas II, in an era of crisis, was there a return to traditional iconography from pseudo-icons. All of the other trends in evolutionary and transient art eventually fell into that abyss into which Roman

Catholic art fell: striving to please the tastes and modes of the "world lying in evil" and taking into contemporary churches the ugliness and abnormality of ultra-modem painting.

The Stoglav Council preserves us from all of these dangers with its traditional "exemplars" of the entire treasury of Eastern Orthodox iconography, which offers material for spiritual "inspiration" and imitation. In the ancient Russian icon we find the highest of artistic expressions of the spiritual apex of Holy Russia's greatest epoch. If in the declining years a servile imitation of foreigners led us to forget these icons, in this twentieth century a renewal of the original Russian culture has begun, and there is a resurgence of an understanding of ancient iconography. We know that war and revolution have halted the growth of this movement and that now in the Russian motherland religious culture is quite suppressed. Thus for us in exile from the motherland our primary responsibility is to recognize and to study the great achievements of our forefathers and to understand that we must end our servile cringing before the West and its materialistic orientation. It is finally time for us to assimilate all that which ancient Orthodox culture, in all of its achievements, manifests in an unsurpassed way in the world of beauty. This is our legacy. We are the heirs and preservers of these treasures. We have no right to disavow this sanctified legacy.[*]

Translated from the Russian by Gregory Telepneff

---

[*] *Orthodox Tradition*, Center for Traditionalist Orthodox Studies, St. Gregory Palamas Monastery, Vol. III, No. 3, 1986 and Vol. IV, No 1, 1987.

An Iconographer's Sketchbook Vol. II

THE TYULIN COLLECTION

LIKE the original Postnikov editions of Volume I, the Tyulin editions do not have any text except the captions on the sketches. In order to avoid repeating the same information in almost every entry, the following information is assumed for each sketch: Icons of our Lord Jesus Christ have His Name abbreviated as "їс хс" which are the first and last letters of the Greek Ἰησοῦς Χριστός written in Slavonic letters. His halo has a three-part cross on which are the letters "о ѿн" which is Greek ὁ ὤν for "THE BEING" or "I AM" written in Slavonic.[1] Icons of the most holy Mother of God have her name in Greek Μήτηρ τοῦ Θεοῦ abbreviated "мѳ ,д.ѵ̈." Generally, in this text, "Богородица" is translated "Theotokos" and "Богоматерь" as "Mother of God." Many icons of the saints are actually inscribed with the original Greek word for "saint" ὁ ἅγιος instead of the Slavonic стый. "The angel of the Lord" translates аггелх гднь or а̃ г̃. As in the church service books, only the first letter is capitalized; in Slavonic the abbreviations are the sign of respect.

The English titles of the sketches generally are translations of the Russian captions which are reprinted in a modern civil typeface. These are followed by the Slavonic titles and texts in a modern Church Slavonic typeface. The Slavonic texts are transcribed and translated independently of the Russian title. The old icons were not inscribed in the standardized Church Slavonic "of the printed books" in which modern icons are usually inscribed. The script on the icons is very often calligraphic with unusual abbreviations and without spaces between the words. However, the inscriptions are generally consistent and it appears the iconographers copied them very carefully from existing icons or from their manuscript pattern books. Every tradition was considered something so sacred that it could not be "touched," even if an error were obviously a handwriting mistake. A number of errors from the manuscript tradition are still found in modern westernized icons. A "|" marks a division in a text. [My additions to texts and conjectures are enclosed in brackets.] In viewing the sketches the following convention must be kept in mind: the lines that form the design are black, but the black patches represent a "bright" area or highlights. The lettering is "bright" red on gold; or perhaps gold or white on a dark color. Originally some sketches had the highlights printed in red ink which did not reproduce well. The sketches are greatly reduced in size from the originals. To avoid

---

[1] The icons should have "ѡ̆" instead of "ѿ." See *An Icon Painter's Notebook*, page 44.

losing the fine lines, they appear "blacker" than the original drawings. The colors and additional information for many of the sketches can be found in *An Icon Painter's Notebook* and *An Iconographer's Patternbook* according to the day of the church year starting in September.

PATTERNS OF OLD RUSSIAN ICONOGRAPHY

1.   The Old Testament Trinity
Ветхозавѣтная Троица

Ст҃а́ѧ тр҃ца

In Genesis 18:1-3 we read, "Then the LORD appeared to him [Abraham] by the terebinth trees of Mamre, as he was sitting in the tent door in the heat of the day. So he lifted his eyes and looked, and behold, three men were standing by him; and when he saw them, he ran from the tent door to meet them, and bowed himself to the ground, and said, 'My Lord, if I have now found favor in Your sight, do not pass on by Your servant.'"(NKJ)

In this text we see a revelation of our Lord Jesus Christ in His pre-Incarnate state. In subsequent chapters it is clear that two of the men were angels who were sent to Sodom and Gomorrah. In previous chapters Abraham had dreams and visions of the Lord and perhaps now he was contemplating his experiences. The text says the LORD appeared to him. When Abraham looked up, three men were there suddenly: he did not hear or see them coming. Abraham addressed the leader, whom he recognized from his vision, with the singular "thou" and the divine title "My Lord." The holy fathers saw a revelation of the Holy Trinity in this passage, even though they did not say the Father or the Holy Spirit appeared personally. This sketch for an icon of the Holy Trinity is called "The Hospitality of Abraham" in Greek. The artistic convention of three young men as a symbolic icon for the Holy Trinity was established in early Christian times. There is an ancient mosaic from about the year 340 of this theme preserved in Saint Mary Major Basilica in Rome. There is a more ancient fresco of the Three Men appearing to Abraham in the catacomb on the Via Latina which is reproduced in this mosaic. The young men are portrayed without beards, wings or halos. Although St. Andrew Rublev's icon of the Holy Trinity has been declared the norm by the Council of a Hundred Chapters in Moscow in 1551, the Greek models are approved by the same decree and include Abraham and Sarah as well. The Holy Trinity feast day is celebrated on Pentecost.

2.   The Old Testament Trinity

In this sketch, as in the first, we see Abraham's tent represented by a palace, the oak of Mamre and the mountain. These are scaled down and the Three Angels are proportionately larger. Two of the Angels appear to be sitting on the table which is set with numerous cups, plates and spoons.

3. **The Savior**
Спаситель
Ї҃с х҃с г҃дь вседержитель

The Russian title given for many icons of our Lord Jesus Christ in these volumes is Спаситель "The Savior." The inscriptions have not been preserved on most of the sketches of Christ. The inscriptions for this icon should be the same as Sketch 1:11. In this sketch we see only the head and part of the shoulders of the Savior. This representation is very popular and can be paired with the "Kazan" Mother of God.

4. **The Savior - Jesus Christ "The Lord Almighty"**
Спаситель - Господь Вседержитель
Ї҃с х҃с г҃дь вседержитель

This is a very traditional depiction of Christ except His hair is flowing down His other shoulder and His tunic and halo are decorated. The inscription on the Gospel book might be Прїидите ко мнѣ вси труждающїися и обремененнїи, и азъ оупокою вы: возмите иго мое на себе и научитеся ѿ мене, ꙗкw кротокъ есмь и смиренъ срцемъ: и wбрящете покой душамъ вашымъ: Иго бо мое благо, и бремя мое легко есть. "Come to Me, all you who labor and are heavy laden, and I will give you rest. Take My yoke upon you and learn from Me, for I am gentle and lowly in heart, and you will find rest for your souls. For My yoke is easy and My burden is light." (Matthew 11: 28-30 NKJ). This icon is also called "The Pantocrator."

5. **Jesus Christ "The Lord Almighty"**
In this variation, the Lord's Gospel book is inscribed, Не на лица судите сынове человѣчестїи но праведенъ. "Do not regard the person; judge the sons of men righteously!" This idea is found throughout the Bible, perhaps not in these exact words.

6. **Jesus Christ "The Lord Almighty"**
This drawing is perhaps the most elegant in its simplicity. There is a humble feeling about it that is very appealing.

7. **The Savior - Jesus Christ "The Lord Almighty"**
Although the previous sketch has more of the feeling of St. Andrew Rublev, the handwriting on the bottom says, "A drawing by Andrew Rublev - Simeon Aaronev." The Gospel text is Matthew 11: 28-30.

8. **Jesus Christ "The Lord Almighty"**
This sketch shows the Lord's hair flowing down on the other shoulder. The blessing hand emerges from a sleeve and the Gospel book is supported on His knee. This

is a portrait icon as if the Lord were sitting down.

9.   Jesus Christ "The Lord Almighty"

This drawing is practically identical to the preceding, except for the guidelines for placing the lettering.

10.   The Savior
Спаситель
Їс҃ х҃с г҃дь вседержи́тель

This is very similar to Sketch 1:3. There is a different feeling about it. Some variations of this icon are called "The Angry Eye."

11.   The Savior - the Lord Almighty
Спаситель
Їс҃ х҃с г҃дь вседержи́тель

This sketch portrays the Lord looking straight at the viewer. This icon is complete with the lettering.

12.   The Savior of Smolensk
Спасъ Смоленцкій
Їс҃ х҃с г҃дь вседержи́тель

Full length icons of our Lord Jesus Christ and the Mother of God are not very common because viewers are more interested in looking at the faces of people. Full length icons must be of monumental size to be recognizable in a large church. This sketch is similar to Sketches 1:25 and 1:27 in Volume I, except the blessing hand is pointing toward the Gospel book. It can be paired with Sketch 2:39 of Vol. I.

13.   Jesus Christ "The Lord Immanuel"
Господь Еммануилъ
Їс҃ х҃с г҃дь є҆мману́илъ

The depiction of a beardless Jesus Christ may be found in early Christian catacomb art, sarcophagi, etc. and was the usual way the Lord was depicted before the iconoclastic controversy. The depiction of Christ as a child began only after the year 1000, when the Christ Child in the disc on the chest of the Icon of most holy Mother of God "The Sign" was taken out of context. (See Vol. I, Sketch 2:16.) Thus, this icon attempts to depict the Second Person of the Holy Trinity before His incarnation. This drawing was probably part of an "Angel Deisis." The Christ Child usually has bright gold robes. This and the following sketches have the proper inscriptions.

14. Jesus Christ "The Lord Immanuel"

This sketch is very decorative. The Christ Child has very curly hair, a wide ornamental band on His tunic and elaborate lettering.

15. The Great High Priest
Великій Архіерей
а́рхїере́й вели́кїй

In Hebrews 4:13-16 we read, "Seeing then that we have a great High Priest who has passed through the heavens, Jesus the Son of God, let us hold fast our confession. For we do not have a High Priest who cannot sympathize with our weaknesses, but was in all points tempted as we are, yet without sin. Let us therefore come boldly to the throne of grace, that we may obtain mercy and find grace to help in time of need. (NKJ)" Our Lord is wearing an ornate bishop's cap, a cross-patterned cloak and omophorion. This icon became common after the fall of Constantinople in 1453. The present sketch depicts only the Lord's head and shoulders, but bust and full-length icons of the "Great High Priest" were common, especially in cathedrals.

16. Image of the Lord "Not Made by Hands"
Нерукотворений Образъ Господень
Сты́й неру́котворе́нїй ѡ́бразъ гд҃а нш҃егѡ і҃са х҃а

When the so-called "Shroud of Turin" was kept in the Imperial Treasury of Constantinople, iconographers were called in to paint what they thought they saw on the fine linen cloth. Since then the features of Christ's face have been standardized and our Lord can be recognized in all subsequent Christian art, both in the east as well as in the west. Most likely when our Lord rose from the dead, the burst of energy scorched the linen and left the faint image which still continues to intrigue scientists and edify the faithful after many centuries of controversy. God, in His infinite wisdom, has arranged that the Shroud can never be proved true or false, so that He will have left physical evidence of the most important event in the Christian faith, but not so overwhelming that faith will no longer be required. Thus, the "Image Not Made by Hands" is actually an icon of the Resurrection of Christ. There are many names for this icon, among which are "The Holy Face," "The Holy Napkin" and "The Mandylion." Two angels of the Lord, each labeled сты́й а́гг҃лъ гд҃нь, are holding the Holy Mandylion. The Lord is avoiding eye contact with the viewer which adds to the mysterious quality of the image of Christ. Variations of this icon have always been very popular and frequently are found painted on the upper margin of icons of saints. Crucifixes, both painted and metal, almost always have the "Image not made by Hands" at the top.

17. The Nativity of Christ
Рождество Христово
Рождество̀ гⷣа нш҃гѡ і҆и҃са хрⷭта̀

The Slavonic inscriptions have not been preserved in our sketch. The traditional elements of the Nativity icon have been arranged differently. The Magi on horseback are pointing to the star, while an unidentified woman with a halo is pointing to the heavenly firmament as well as pointing to the Infant in the manger. Three angels are kneeling before the Child while a fourth angel is speaking to the shepherd blowing a horn. (An outstretched hand is an artistic convention indication the person is speaking. Orators traditionally extended one arm for emphasis.) The Infant is watched over by the ox and donkey. While the Mother of God looks on, an old shepherd is reassuring St. Joseph the Betrothed by telling him about the shepherds' experience with the angels and the message they were given. Below the midwives are washing the Newborn while another shepherd is feeding and petting his sheep. This sketch is a charming example of folk iconography.

18. The Circumcision of the Lord and St. Basil the Great
Обрѣзаніе Господне и Василій Великій
Ѡ҆брѣзанїе гⷣа на́шегѡ і҆и҃са хрⷭта̀ | ст҃ый василїй вели́кїй

In Luke 2:21 we read, "And when eight days were completed for the circumcision of the Child, His name was called Jesus, the name given by the angel before He was conceived in the womb. (NKJ)" In the sketch we see ст҃ый і҆ѡ́сифъ Saint Joseph and the Mother of God presenting the Christ Child to ст҃ый прⷪ́рокъ заха́рїа the holy prophet Zachariah in the Temple. Although January 1 is an important feast day on which the Divine Liturgy is always celebrated, icons for this day are exceedingly rare. January 1 is also the feast day of St. Basil the Great who is standing in an archway. The drawing of St. Basil is a model for other saints.

19. The Meeting of the Lord
Срѣтеніе Господне
Срⷮѣтенїе гⷣа на́шегѡ і҆и҃са хрⷭта̀

This feast day, also known as "The Presentation of our Lord in the Temple," falls forty days after Christmas on February 2. Behind the most holy Mother of God, St. Joseph the Betrothed is holding a cage with the doves not depicted here. St. Simeon the God-bearer is holding the Christ Child and behind them St. Anna the Prophetess is holding a scroll. Behind them is a palace representing the Temple in Jerusalem with the Altar.

20. Mid-Pentecost or the Twelve-year-old Jesus Christ in the Temple
Преполовеніе или 12ᵀᴴ лѣтній ІС ХС во Храмѣ.
Преполове́ніе

Mid-Pentecost is the feast day marking the halfway point between Pascha and Pentecost and is celebrated on the Wednesday before the Sunday of the Samaritan woman. The Gospel reading for that day begins, "Now about the middle of the feast Jesus went up into the temple and taught." John 7:14 (NKJ) The theme of the service is "The Living Water" to prepare us for the Gospel about the woman at the well to be read the following Sunday. The icon depicts St. Luke 2:41-52 about the time when Jesus' parents took Him to Jerusalem when He was twelve years old. He was left behind and three days they found Him in the temple, sitting in the midst of the teachers, both listening to them and asking them questions. Saint Joseph ст҃ый іѡсифъ and the Mother of God are standing on the left side of the icon with their hands raised indicating they are speaking. Jesus is shown as a beardless youth teaching the doctors of the law from a book. Completed icons have diverse inscriptions, among which are "Mid-feast" and "The Lord Conversing with the Scribes."

21. The Transfiguration of the Lord
Преображеніе Господне
Преѡбраже́ніе гд҃а нш҃гѡ і҃иса хр҃та

Matthew 17:1-3 says, "Jesus took Peter, James, and John his brother, led them up on a high mountain by themselves; and He was transfigured before them. His face shone like the sun, and His clothes became as white as the light. And behold, Moses and Elijah appeared to them, talking with Him." (NKJ) Our sketch shows the Lord speaking to Peter James and John and leading them up the mountain on the right side of the drawing. In the upper left-hand corner we see an angel bringing the holy prophet Elias in a cloud. On the upper right-hand corner we see an angel bringing Moses out of his tomb. In the center we have the actual event of the Transfiguration. Our Lord Jesus Christ is in a circular cloud raising His right hand in blessing and holding a scroll in His left. Three large rays of light are emanating from Christ to the apostles below. On the left Elias is holding his hands in prayer and on the right Moses is holding the tablets of the Law. Below we see the three apostles: from the left John, James and Peter overcome by the revelation of Jesus Christ's divine nature. On the left we see them descending from the mountain and Christ has his hand raised. The icon of the Transfiguration is blessed as an icon of the Holy Trinity: God the Father is invisible, but His voice was heard; The Son is our Lord Jesus Christ, and the Holy Spirit is represented by the cloud.

22. The Entrance into Jerusalem

Входъ Господень во Їерусалимъ

Вхо́дъ во іеру́салймъ гⷣа нш҃гⱳ і҃и҃са хрⷭ҇та̀

This is a typical and straightforward design for the Palm Sunday icon.

23. The Eucharist

Евхаристія

Прїими́те, ꙗди́те, сїѐ є҆́сть тⷯѣ́ло моѐ

The inscription at the top says, "Take, eat, this is My body." The Lord is giving St. Peter a portion of the Holy Eucharist from the bowl on the altar. Five more apostles are behind him. Notice the chalice on the right edge of the altar and the baldachin over the Lord. This icon is one of a pair very often placed over the royal doors to the altar.

24. The Eucharist

Евхаристія

Пі́йте ѿ неѧ̀ вси̑, сїѧ̀ є҆́сть кро́вь моѧ̀ ꙗже за вы̀ и҆злива́емаѧ во ѡ҆ставле́нїе грⷯѣ́хⱳⷡ҇въ.

The inscription at the top says, "All drink of this, this is My blood which is shed for you for the forgiveness of sins." Instead of a chalice our Lord is extending a bottle to the Apostle Paul and the five others behind him. Notice the Gospel book on the altar.[2]

25. The Crucifixion

Паспятіе Господне

Распѧ́тїе гⷣа бг҃а нш҃гⱳ і҃и҃са хрⷭ҇та̀

The Slavonic inscription says, "The Crucifixion of our Lord God Jesus Christ." The title board on the Cross says, ца́рь сла́вы "The King of Glory." The men on the right are marked і҆ⱳа́ннъ John, and ло́ггінъ Longinus. The walls of Jerusalem have an ornamental motif.

26. The Crucifixion

We see a mountain, with Christ crucified on it; on either side of Him are the two thieves. The one on the right, with a rounded beard and grey hair, says to Christ, "Remember me, Lord, when You come into Your kingdom." The one on the left, a beardless young man, turns away and says: "If You are the Christ, save Yourself and us." On the top of Christ's cross is a tablet marked with the initials **INBI** for "Jesus of Nazareth, King of the Jews" in Greek. Below the cross is a small cavity in which are Adam's skull and two bones,

---

[2] Sketch 1:24 is missing from the copies of the original available. It is replaced with this drawing from Pokrovsky, page 15.

sprinkled with the blood of Christ that runs from the wounds in His feet.[3] In this sketch the Mother of God and the walls of Jerusalem are omitted. Above are two angels weeping for Christ and above Him is the "Lord of Sabaoth."

27. Taking our Lord Jesus Christ Down from the Cross
Снятіе со Креста Господа Нашего Іисуса Христа
Снѧ́тїе съ крⷭ҇та̀ гдⷭ҇а бг҃а нш҃гѡ і҆и҃са хрⷭ҇та̀

A ladder is leaning against the Cross. і҆ѡ́сифъ ѿ а҆рїма́д,е́а Joseph of Arimathea is holding Christ around the waist; The Mother of God is standing on a stool and holding His shoulders; St. John the Theologian is holding His legs and нїкоди́мъ Nicodemus is pulling out the nails. The holy myrrh-bearing women are lamenting the death of Christ while Adam's skull is next to Nicodemus' leg.

28. The Resurrection of Christ
Воскресеніе Христово
Воскресе́нїе хрⷭ҇то́во

The inscriptions have not been preserved on this sketch, which shows the traditional "Harrowing of Hades" Our Lord Jesus Christ is standing on the bronze gates of hell in a glorious aureole. He is pulling Adam from the tomb by his wrist as one would grasp a corpse. If Christ were raising a living person, He would have grasped his hand and fingers. Above Christ are two angels. Behind Adam are Kings David and Solomon, Daniel, a prophet, and John the Forerunner. On the right side Eve is rising from her tomb; above her are the prophets Moses, Jonah, Isaiah, Jeremiah and others. Below on the left two angels are harassing an old man personifying Hades and on the right Jesus is stepping out of the tomb while the guards are asleep around it.

29. "Only Begotten Son and Word of God"
Единородный Сине и Слово Божіе
Е҆диноро́дныи сн҃е и҆ сло́ве бж҃їй

This icon is supposed to illustrate the dogmatic hymn sung at the Divine Liturgy to conclude the Second Antiphon. At the top middle field dividing the title of the icon, "O Only Begotten Son and Word of God," we see the Lord Sabaoth in a circle and Jesus Christ "Immanuel" sitting on seraphim, holding a scroll in His left hand and an eight-pointed star containing a dove representing the Holy Spirit. On the left side the Mother of God is sitting on a throne and has the Christ Child standing on her lap. On the right side Ss. Basil the Great, John Chrysostom and Gregory the Theologian are standing with an angel behind an altar with a chalice. The two middle angels are kneeling in prayer to

---

[3] Hetherington, page 38.

10

the Holy Trinity before them. Below them in the center is a depiction of "Do not weep for Me, Mother." The line extending from Christ's mouth to the lower right side is a probably a printing flaw. Christ is portrayed as a soldier sitting leisurely on a three-barred cross holding a sword. His halo is marked with the о ѿн. An angel is about to strike someone lying on his back with his throat bared and arms crossed. A demon is driving some strange nude beings into the abyss. Opposite them a seraph with a sword is over a nude man on a demonic horse (notice the birds' feet instead of hooves) with a spear and a basket on his shoulder. The horseman is trampling a number of what appear to be corpses. This is an example of a fantasy icon with a clutter of figures which can only confuse the viewer.

30. Deisis - Деисисъ
30 a. The Mother of God
30 b. Jesus Christ "The Lord Almighty"
30 c. St. John the Forerunner

In the original Tyulin these three separate icons were placed on one page to form a deisis group. The most holy Mother of God holds her hands in prayer. The Savior is holding a Gospel book which says, Нє на лицà зрàщє сҮдѝтє сы́новє человѣ́чєстïн но прáвєдєнх. "Do not regard the person; judge the sons of men righteously." St. John is pointing to a bowl containing the Christ Child which is a very graphic representation of the Most Holy Eucharist. He is holding a scroll Сè, áгнєцх бж҃ïй, взє́млай грѣхѝ мírа. покáнтєса, прнблнжн во са цр҃твïє нб҃ноє. "Behold! The Lamb of God who takes away the sins of the world! Repent, for the kingdom of heaven is at hand!" (John 1:29; Matthew 3:1 NKJ).

31. Deisis - Деисисъ
31 a. St. Peter, St. Michael and the Mother of God
31 b. Jesus Christ
31 c. St. John the Forerunner, St. Gabriel and St. Paul

The drawings of these seven separate deisis icons were assembled to make one large page on the original Tyulin. The central icon of our Lord interests us the most. Our Lord Jesus Christ is sitting on a throne in an oval containing an eight-pointed star, a reminder of the eighth day of eternity. In the four corners are the symbols of the evangelists and around Him are a multitude of cherubim. This representation of Christ is of the last judgement and His Gospel book may be opened to Matthew 25:31 and following, "When the Son of Man comes in His glory, and all the holy angels with Him..."

32. The "King of Kings" or "The Queen Stood"
Царь Царемъ или Предста Царица
Предста царица

Psalm 44:10 says, "The queen stood at Your right hand, dressed in a golden robe with many colors." Our Lord Jesus Christ is portrayed as the Great High Priest blessing and holding a closed Gospel book and a thin scepter. On His right the Mother of God is dressed in a very elaborate royal robe and wearing a crown as the queen of heaven. Opposite is St. John the Forerunner dressed in his usual fur tunic and cloth cloak. Above the throne are С҃тый мїхаилъ а҆рхаг҃глъ the holy Archangel Michael and С҃тый гаврїилъ а҆рхаг҃глъ the holy Archangel Gabriel.

33. Jesus Christ "Do Not Weep for Me, Mother"
Не Рыдай Мене Мати
Оу҆ны́нїе г҃да на́шегѡ і҆и҃са х҃рта̀

The Slavonic inscription says, "The Lamentation of our Lord Jesus Christ." Our Lord Jesus Christ, having been taken down from the Cross, is shown standing in the tomb being caressed by His most pure Mother. His hands are crossed over His abdomen like the Figure on the Shroud of Turin.

34. The "Akhremsky" Icon of the Mother of God
Ахремская Икона Б. М.
О́бразъ прест҃ы́я бц҃ы а҆хремскїя

The "Yakhromsky" or "Akhrensky" Icon appeared on October 14, 1482 at St. Cosmas Men's Monastery in the Diocese of Vladimir. The Mother of God is holding the Christ Child together with a scroll in her right hand. The handwriting at the bottom says, "Copy taken in black from the Akhremsky Image of the most holy Theotokos." The illustration in Poselyanin shows an entirely different icon and he gives two different spellings.

35. The "Bogolyubsky" Icon of the Mother of God
Боголюбская Икона Б. М.
О́бразъ прест҃ы́я бц҃ы бг҃олюбскїя

The title of the icon means "Beloved of God," the surname of the Russian Prince St. Andrew of Vladimir whose day is July 4. The most holy Mother of God is facing the Savior in the clouds. Kneeling before her in prayer is the holy Prince Andrew Bogolyubsky celebrated June 29 and July 4. He is identified by the Slavonic inscription: С҃тый кна́зъ а҆ндре́й бг҃олюбскїй. The "Bogolyubsky" icon is celebrated on June 18 and has many variations. The original icon had no saints.

36. **The Icon of the Mother of God "The Child Leapt"**
Икона Б. М. Взыгранiе
Взыгра́нїе младе́нца

This icon appeared on November 7, 1795 and has several variations. In this one the Mother of God is facing left.

37. **The Icon of the Mother of God "The Child Leapt"**

In this variation the Child is in the same position holding the scroll, but the Mother of God is facing right.

38. **The "Georgian" Icon of the Mother of God**
Грузинская Икона Б. М.
О́бразъ прест҃ы́а бц҃ы гр꙼зинскїа

This icon takes its name from an icon Gregory Lytkin, a business man from Yaroslav, purchased in Georgia and which was placed in the Krasnogorsky Monastery in Archangelsk. It is celebrated on August 22.

39. **The "Dnieper" Icon of the Mother of God**
Днѣпрская Икона Б. М.
О́бразъ прест҃ы́а бц҃ы каспершвскїа

Poselyanin does not list a "Dnieper" icon. What the editors named after the Dnieper River in Ukraine appears to be a variation of the "Casperov" or "Korsun" icon of the Mother of God. The Christ Child has a scroll in His hand under His mother's chin. The icon is celebrated on October 1 and June 29.

40. **The Image of the Most Holy Theotokos "The Sign"**
Образъ Пресвя. Богор. Знаменiе
О́бразъ прест҃ы́а бц҃ы зна́менїе

This sketch omits the stars, lettering and decorative features of Vol. I, Sketch 2:16.

41. **The "Iveron" Icon of the Mother of God**
Иверская Икона Б. М.
О́бразъ прест҃ы́а бц҃ы і́верскїа

This is the miracle working icon of the Mother of God "Portaitissa" in the Iveron (Iberian) Monastery on Mount Athos. A copy of the icon was taken to Moscow in the year 1647 and placed by Tsar Alexis and Patriarch Nicon in the chapel of the Resurrection Gate. This icon is a classic "Hodegetria" and in its many variations is very often one of the main icons of the iconostasis in a church. Sometimes there is a bleeding flesh wound on the Virgin's right cheek as on the original icon on the Holy Mountain. A Saracen cut the icon with his sword, which caused the icon to bleed. The icon is celebrated on the Tuesday of Bright Week, on February 12 and October 13.

42. Icon of the Mother of God "The Uncut Stone"

Икона Б. М. Камень Нерукосѣчний

Ѻ҆бразъ престы́а бц҃ы камень нерꙋкосѣ́чный

See the commentary to Sketch 2:23 in Vol. I. The "Stone" or "Rock" is Jesus Christ, who was born of the Virgin Mary, the most holy Mother of God. In this icon we see the Mother of God with three women's faces in circles replacing the usual stars. Her robe is covered with meandering lines representing clouds which are overshadowing a stylized mountain. On her breast are "Jacob's Ladder," a pillar, and Christ the King.

43. The "Modensky" Icon of the Mother of God

Моденская Икона Б. М.

Ѻ҆бразъ престы́а бц҃ы моденскі́а

Count Boris Sheremetiev purchased the original icon in Modena, Italy in 1717 and brought it back to Russia where many miracles took place by God's grace. It is celebrated on June 20.

44. Icon of the Mother of God "Unexpected Joy"

Икона Б. М. Нечаянная Радость

Ѻ҆бразъ престы́а бц҃ы нечаа́нїа ра́дости

Some icons have a tablet on which is written, "A certain sinful man had great devotion to the most holy Theotokos to whom he prayed diligently everyday, and after praying went out to sin. One day while he was praying to the Theotokos, he saw the figures in the icon move. Wounds in the Child's hands, feet and side began to bleed. And he asked the icon, 'O Lady, who did this?' She answered him, 'You and other sinners crucify Him all the time like the Jews did.'"[4] At once the man saw the destructive nature of his sinful life and received the "unexpected joy" of true repentance and forgiveness. In our sketch we see the man praying before the Mother of God and the Christ Child is showing His wounds. There are many variations of and feast days for this icon, the principal being December 9.

---

[4] Translated from plate 210-211 in Timchenko.

45. Icon of the Mother of God "O, All-hymned Mother"
Икона Б. М. О Всепѣтая Мати
Ѻбразъ престыѧ бцы ѽ всепѣтаѧ мтн

The last kontakion of the Akathist Hymn reads, "O all-hymned Mother, who gave birth to [God] the Word holier than all the saints, now accept our offering, save from every misfortune and rescue from future punishment all those who sing to you: Alleluia!"[5] The Mother of God is holding the Christ Child on her knees. She is wearing a large crown and has women's heads on her robe instead of stars. The Christ Child is not wearing a tunic. Poselyanin does not give any information about this icon other than the day, October 6.

46. The "Petrov" Icon of the Mother of God
Петровская Икона Б. М.
Ѻбразъ престыѧ бцы петровскіѧ

This icon is named in honor of Metropolitan Peter of Moscow, who painted the original. It is commemorated on April 24.

47. The "Smolensk" Icon of the Mother of God
Смоленская Икона Б. М.
Ѻбразъ Престыѧ бцы смоленскіѧ

Volume I has a number of icons named "Smolensk." This variation shows the Christ Child looking away from the viewer, unlike the others.

48. The "Shuisko-Smolensk" Icon of the Mother of God
Шуйско-Смоленская Икона Б. М.
Ѻбразъ Престыѧ бцы смоленскіѧ

Poselyanin calls this the "Hodegetria from Shui" icon celebrated on November 1. It is unusual because the Child is holding His chin and foot. "A Short Explanation of the Miracle Working Icon of Smolensk" lists 37 cures from eye problems, 15 exorcisms, 13 foot problems, seven ear problems, seven from internal disorders, seven from weakness, five from migraine, and 24 cures of various ailments.

49. The "Passion" Icon of the Mother of God
Страстная Икона Б. М.
Ѻбразъ престыѧ бцы страстніѧ

This is a mirror image of an original icon created by Andreas Ricco. It received the title "Passion" from the two angels who are depicted holding the instruments related to the

---

[5] *Large Prayerbook*, page 533.

Passion of our Lord Jesus Christ. On the top right the holy Archangel Gabriel is holding the lance and the reed with a sponge and on the top left St. Michael the Archangel is holding the Cross. Other versions add the crown of thorns, the nails, the container of vinegar, etc. Notice the floral decoration on the Virgin's head covering. The "Passion" Icon is celebrated on August 13. At least five of these icons were well-known in Russia at the turn of the century.

50. Icon of the Mother of God "Of Three Joys"
Икона Б. М. Трехъ Радостей
Ѻбразъ трехъ радостей

Poselyanin tells us on page 770 that at the beginning of the eighteenth century a pious artist brought from Italy a picture of the Holy Family. The Mother of God is holding the Child on her knees while the young St. John the Forerunner has his hands held in prayer. The іѡсифъ правє Righteous Joseph is on the left. Notice the Family is inside a room, rather than in front of a palace as is customary in icons.

51. "Praises of the Most Holy Theotokos"
Похвала Пресвятыя Богородицы
Похвалы престыя бцы

The "Praises of the Most Holy Theotokos" is another name for the Akathist Hymn sung on the fifth Saturday of Great Lent. From top to bottom in the middle field of the icon we see Christ "Immanuel" and the most holy Mother of God on a throne surrounded by a floral garland. Barlaam is underneath. On the left from the top down are the holy prophets Habbakuk, Nahum, Zachariah (the father of the Forerunner), Moses, Solomon, and David. On the right are Zachariah, Elias, Daniel, Elisha, Jeremiah and Gideon holding the fleece. There are, of course, many possibilities to develop this icon. For example, it should have Isaiah holding a scroll that says, "A Virgin will conceive and bear a Son." In various places one can find texts for the scrolls. For example: Habbakuk's scroll can say, "God will come from the east, and the Holy One from the overshadowed mountains." Nahum's scroll can say, "I saw you the true vineyard, from which has grown the vine of life which is Christ." Zachariah's scroll can say, "'Blessed is the God of Israel for He has met and created the salvation of His people." Moses' scroll can say, "I saw the burning bush which was not consumed." Solomon's scroll can say, "Wisdom has built herself a temple and strengthened it with seven pillars, and offered her sacrifices." David's scroll can say, "Rise up, O Lord, in Your rest, You and the tabernacle of Your sanctuary!" Zachariah's scroll can say, "Rejoice exceedingly, O daughters of Sion!" Elias' scroll can say, "I was very zealous for the Lord Almighty." Daniel's scroll can say, "I saw a great mountain from which came the rock which was hewn without being touched by human hands." Elisha's scroll can say, "Elisha said, 'Whom do you seek? Go, follow him!'"

Jeremiah's scroll can say "I have seen you, O Israel, the hand leading the holy child along the path of life." Gideon's can say, I saw you as a fleece, O pure Virgin, for I saw the miracle of your offspring in the fleece. Barlaam's can say, "A Star will come out of Jacob, a Scepter will rise out of Israel. (Num. 24:17)"[6]

52. The Nativity of the Mother of God
Рождество Б. М.
Рождество престтыѧ бцы

On the left we see the usual depiction of the Birth of the Mother of God. Two maids are waiting on St. Anna. To the right we see Ss. Joachim and Anna holding and rejoicing over the birth of Mary. In the lower left-hand corner we see the maids bathing the infant Mary. Above we see Joachim looking on through a window.

53. The Nativity of the Mother of God
This is a slightly more ornate version of the basic icon. The Church celebrates this feast on September 8.

54. The Annunciation of the Mother of God
Благовѣщеніе Б. М.
Благовѣщеніе престтыѧ бцы

We see the Archangel Gabriel announcing to the Virgin Mary that she would be the Mother of God. This is the basic design for an icon of the Annunciation celebrated on March 25.

55. The Dormition of the Theotokos
Успеніе Пресв. Богородицы
Оуспеніе престтыѧ бцы

In the center we see Jesus Christ in an aureole surrounded by angels and seraphim holding the soul of the Mother of God who is laid out on a bier surrounded by the twelve apostles and others. In front St. Michael the Archangel is cutting off the hands of the blasphemer Athon. In the center the Mother of God is on a throne in an aureole being carried up to the heavenly sphere. The twelve apostles are being transported on clouds to participate in her Dormition. The Dormition or "Assumption" is celebrated on August 15.

---

[6] *An Icon Painter's Notebook*, page 26.

56. St. Michael the Archangel
Св. Михаилъ Архангелъ
Ст҃ый мїхаи́лъ а҆рха́гг҃лъ

St. Michael is shown in very rich deacons' vestments; the orarion and hems are embroidered with seraphim. He is surrounded by angels standing on a royal cushion holding a staff in his right-hand and a disk depicting the Synaxis of Angels with the Ancient of Days in his lefthand. To our right we see these same angels driving sinners into the jaws of hell. On the lower left-hand corner is the Miracle of Colossae with the monastic St. Archippus celebrated on September 6. The overabundance of details that would distract the parishioners make this design unsuitable for an icon that will be venerated in church on St. Michael's day, November 8.

57. The Guardian Angel
Ангелъ Хранитель
о҆ а҆гі́осъ а҆́гг҃лъ храни́тель

Under the "Image not made by human hands" the angel is standing on a cloud holding a sword in his left hand. In his right hand is a cross marked "The Cross of the Lord protects me by night."

58. The Holy Guardian Angel
The Guardian angel is standing on clouds in an elaborate landscape. He is holding a cross in his right hand which was omitted from the sketch and a sword in his left. A disk with the Lord Immanuel is on his chest.

59. St. John the Forerunner
Св. Їоаннъ Предтеча
Ст҃ый і҆ѡа́ннъ предте́ча

This sketch could be used to design an icon for a deisis group. St. John's fur tunic usually is painted a blue-gray and his cloak may be green.

60. St. John the Forerunner
St. John appears to be blessing with both hands. It is unusual for the Forerunner to be depicted without a tunic.

61. St. John the Forerunner
The title at the top says, "і҆і хі - The Decapitation of the Venerable Head of St. John the Forerunner." He is standing on a mountain with the Jordan River (потомо́съ is Greek for "river" written in Slavonic letters) flowing down it. Notice the starry firmament and the tree with the axe in it.

18

62. St. John the Forerunner

Here we see the Forerunner in prayer before the Ancient of Days on a throne surrounded by angels in a cloud. The wilderness of the great Russian forests was the equivalent of the desert. We see a diminutive St. John praying in the desert, and a young St. John being led by an angel.

63. The Beheading of John the Forerunner
Усѣкновеніе Главы Іоанна Предтеча
Оу҆сѣкновеніе честны́а главы̀ ст҃а́гѡ і҆ѡа́нна предте́чи

The Decapitation of St. John the Forerunner is on August 29. The Savior accompanied by an angel of the Lord is at the top. St. John is being led from the prison by a soldier. In the center the Saint is being beheaded and his head is resting in a bowl in an abyss. Notice that the Forerunner is not wearing a cloak.

64. The Beheading of St. John the Forerunner

This is a more elaborate depiction of the Decapitation of St. John the Forerunner. In the upper left-hand corner the Saint is in prison praying to the Ancient of Days in the clouds above. An angel is speaking to St. John. On the right side we see Salome dancing at Herod's birthday celebration. In the lower left-hand corner we see St. John being led to execution. In the center is the actual beheading and St. John's headless body lies below. On the right we see the soldier presenting the head of St. John to Salome.

65. The Synaxis of St. John the Forerunner
Соборъ Іоаннъ Предтеча
Собо́рх і҆ѡа́нна предте́чи и҆ крести́тела гд҃на

We see St. John baptizing some men in the Jordan River while the scribes and Pharisees are discussing this among themselves. Above is the "Kazan" Icon of the Mother of God in the clouds. The Synaxis of St. John is observed on January 7.

66. Ss. John the Forerunner, John Chrysostom and the Martyr Nikita
Св. Іоаннъ Предтеча, Іоаннъ Златоустъ и Муч. Никита
Ст҃ы́й і҆ѡа́ннх предте́ча, ст҃ы́й і҆ѡа́ннх златоу́стх, ст҃ы́й мꙋ́ченикх ні́кита.

This was perhaps an icon of the favorite saints of a particular family. St. John the Baptist is holding a staff, a bowl with his head marked with his name, and a scroll "Repent, for the kingdom of God..." St. John Chrysostom is wearing a many-crossed cloak and is holding the Gospel book. He is commemorated on November 13, January 27 and 30. The holy martyr Nikita is holding a spear and a cross, and is commemorated on September 15.

67. Holy Forefather Jacob

Св. Праотецъ Їаковъ

Ст҃ый пра́ѻтецъ і́аковъ

This appears to be an icon from the tier of the forefathers on a complete iconostasis. St. Jacob is depicted in a blue tunic and an ocher cloak and blessing. His scroll says, а҃зъ постнꙋю сказалъ лѣтовъ "I | fasting | said | of years." This cryptic saying is best replaced with the customary "There will not lack a prince from among the Jews and an elder from his flesh, until the Lord comes."[7]

68. Holy Prophet Elias

Св. Пророкъ Илія

Ст҃ый прⷬокъ и҆лїа

The inscription should say, "The Fiery Ascent of the Prophet of God Elias." Below and to the left Elisha is looking up to Elias and catching the mantle which is falling from heaven. In the middle we see Elisha and Elias about to cross the Jordan River. To the right in the middle Elias is sitting in his cave and below he is being fed by an angel while asleep.

69. St. Simeon the God-bearer

Св. Симеонъ Богопріимецъ

Ст҃ый сѷмеѻ́нъ бг҃опрїи́мецъ

This icon is a detail from the icon of the Meeting of the Lord.

70. The Holy Prophetess Anna

Св. Пророчица Анна

Ст҃а́а а́нна прⷬочица

This is the prophetess Anna who was present at the Meeting of the Lord in the Temple. She is among the most popular saints after whom many women and sisterhoods are named. She is wearing a very decorative maphorion while holding a cross and scroll.

71. St. John the Theologian

Їоаннъ Богословъ

Ст҃ый і҆ѡа́ннъ бг҃осло́въ

St. John is opening the Gospel to the words, "In the beginning..." He is holding an inkwell and pen box in the crook of his arm. An angel with an eight-pointed star in his halo is whispering into the ear of the Theologian. St. John is commemorated on September 26, May 8 and June 30.

---

[7] An Icon Painter's Notebook, page 26.

72. St. John the Theologian

This sketch is very similar to the first except the Gospel book is opened to въ началѣ бѣ слово, и слово бѣ къ бгꙋ, и бгъ бѣ слово. "In the beginning was the Word, and the Word was with God, and the Word was God." (John 1:1 NKJ) Here St. John is touching his lips as a sign of silence.

73. Ss. Peter and Paul, Apostles
Св. Апостолы Петръ и Павелъ
стый аплъ петръ | стый аплъ павелъ

This is a fine full-length portrait icon with our Lord Jesus Christ Immanuel. St. Peter is holding a scroll and a key; St. Paul is holding a Gospel book. Ss. Peter and Paul are celebrated on June 29.

74. Ss. Peter and Paul, Apostles

Here the Apostles are praying before the Lord Immanuel who is blessing with both hands. Peter is holding a scroll which says, ты еси петръ, и на семъ камени созижду црковъ мою "You are Peter and on this rock I will build My Church." Matthew 16:18.

75. St. Leontius of Rostov the Miracle Worker
Св. Леонтій Ростовскій Чуд.
стый леонтій ростовскій чꙋдотворецъ

St. Leontius was born in Kiev and traveled to Constantinople. He returned to Kiev and became a monk at the Pecherska Lavra Monastery and later became bishop of Rostov. He died in 1070 and his incorrupt relics were opened by Prince Andrew Bogolyubsky in 1112. The Lord Immanuel is in the clouds above the Saint who is blessing with one hand and holding the Gospel with the other. Holding objects in a cloth is a gesture of the greatest respect taken over from Byzantine imperial court ceremonies. He is wearing the white cowl while his phelonion is decorated with a circular motif and a floral lining. This design would make a very impressive icon. St. Leontius is commemorated on May 23.

76. St. Nikita of Novgorod the Miracle Worker
Св. Никита Новгородскій Чуд.
стый нікита новгородскій

St. Nikita was originally a monk of the Pecherska Lavra in Kiev. He is standing in prayer before Christ and is wearing a bishop's cap. He did not have a beard. He died in 1108 and was glorified as a saint in 1558. He is commemorated on January 31 and April 30.

77. The Holy Metropolitan Jonah
Св. Митрополитъ Їона
Ст҃ый і҆ѡ́на

Hierarch Jonah, Metropolitan of Kiev and Vladimir, Miracle worker of Moscow died in 1461. He is shown here on a decorative carpet praying before the Savior. He is wearing a white cowl, very ornate vestments and both hands are held up in prayer.

78. The Holy Metropolitan Alexis and Monastic St. Simeon.
Св. Митроп. Алексѣй и Преп. Симеонъ
Ст҃ый а҆ле́ѯїй митрополі́тъ; | препода́бный сѷмеѡ́нъ

Christ the Savior is blessing from His heavenly sphere. Hierarch Alexis of Moscow, Metropolitan of Kiev and Vladimir lived from 1300 to 1378. He is wearing a richly brocaded saccos and a cowl. He is celebrated on February 12, May 20 and October 5. It is not clear which monastic St. Simeon is depicted here.

79. The Three Hierarchs: Ss. John Chrysostom, Basil the Great and Gregory the Theologian
Три Святителя Василій Вел. Їоаннъ Злат. и Григорій Богос.
ст҃ый григо́рїй бг҃осла́въ | ст҃ый васі́лїй вели́кїй | ст҃ый і҆ѡ́ннъ зла́тоѹстъ

St. Gregory the Theologian is commemorated on January 25; St. Basil the Great on January 1 and St. John Chrysostom is commemorated on November 13 and January 27. They are celebrated together on January 30. Our sketch shows them wearing richly decorated vestments.

80. The Three Hierarchs: Ss. John Chrysostom, Basil the Great and Gregory the Theologian

They are shown in prayer before our Lord Jesus Christ represented by the Mandylion.

81. St. Nicholas the Miracle Worker
Св. Николай Чудотв.
ст҃ый никола́й чѹдотво́рецъ

St. Nicholas is shown holding the Gospel book with both hands. This icon is unique in that it has his omophorion passing over itself rather than under. St. Nicholas is celebrated on December 6 and May 9.

82. St. Nicholas the Miracle Worker

This is a variation of the following sketch.

83. St. Nicholas the Miracle Worker

St. Nicholas of Myra in Lycia is probably the most popular saint of all time. The inscriptions usually have St. Nicholas' name in the vocative case form Нїко́лае "Nicholas!" instead of the nominative or subject form Нїкола́й Nicholas.

84. Ss. Athanasius and Makarius of Alexandria and Nicholas the Miracle Worker
Св. Аѳанасій и Макарій Александр. и Николай Чуд.
Сті҃ый мака́рїй алеѯандрі́нскїй | сті҃ый нїкола́й чꙋд. | сті҃ый патрїа́рхъ а҆ѳана́сїй

The Slavonic inscription reads, "St. Makarius of Alexandria, St. Nicholas the Miracle Worker, St. Patriarch Athanasius." There are, in fact, two saints named Makarius of Alexandria: both are monastics. One is depicted in monastic robes, the other nude. They are celebrated on January 19. Saints Cyril and Athanasius of Alexandria are celebrated on January 18. Both are bishops. I suspect the iconographer painted "Makarius" instead of "Cyril." Also, St. Cyril is distinguished by his bishop's cap.[8] Therefore, the icon should be titled from left to right "St. Athanasius of Alexandria, St. Nicholas the Miracle Worker, St. Cyril of Alexandria."

85. Holy Great Martyr Demetrius, Nicholas the Miracle Worker, and Ignatius the God-bearer
Св. Вм. Димитрій, Николай Чуд. и Игнатій Богоносецъ
Сті҃ый вл҃комч҃никъ димн́трїй | сті҃ый николай чꙋдотво́рецъ | сті҃ый і҆гна́тїй бг҃оно́сецъ

St. Demetrius is standing very calmly while holding a sword and a lance. He is commemorated on October 26. St. Nicholas is standing on a cathedra in front of what may be an altar. The outlined crosses are black or dark. The last figure is an unspecified monastic St. Ignatius. St. Ignatius the God-bearer, the Archbishop of Antioch, is always portrayed as a bishop. His days are December 20 and January 29.

86. St. Demetrius of Thessalonica
Св. Димитрій Солунскій
Сті҃ый великомч҃никъ димн́трїй мѷрото́чецъ

Please see the commentary in Vol. I, Sketch 2:59, page 42. Concerning the angel with the two maidens on the right side: Barbarians captured two young women who were skilled in embroidery work and gave them to their prince. The prince wanted an image of St. Demetrius embroidered for him, but they did not want to make one because they feared the Prince would worship it and thus dishonor the Saint. The prince threatened them with death, so they prayed to St. Demetrius to rescue them from their plight. They completed the work on October 26, the Saint's feast day. After they wept and fell asleep

---

[8] See *Stroganov* page 193.

over their embroidery, the Saint suddenly took them back to Thessalonica and left them and the embroidery at his tomb in his church during the vigil service. The people there were amazed when they saw this miracle. When the maidens awoke, they said, "Glory to God! Where are we?" They thought they were dreaming, but when they saw the tomb of the saint and the people, they understood they were in Thessalonica. They thanked St. Demetrius for interceding with God for the miracle. His embroidered image was placed above the altar, and through it many miracles were worked, to the glory of God.[9]

87. St. Demetrius of Thessalonica

Here St. Demetrius is sitting on a throne holding a staff surmounted with a cross and holding a shield in the left. A lion is under his feet.

88. Holy Martyrs Gurias, Samonas and Abibus
Св. Муч. Гурій, Самонъ и Авивъ
Стый мⷱникⷮ гꙋрій | стый мⷱникⷮ самѡⷩⷯ| стый мⷱникⷮ авіⷡⷯ
These holy martyrs died in the year 306 and are celebrated on November 15.

89. Holy Martyrs Cosmas and Damian
Св. Муч. Козьма и Даміанъ
Стый мⷱникⷮ безсребникⷮ козмà | і҃с х҃с | Стый мⷱникⷮ безсребникⷮ даміанⷮ
There are several pairs of saints named Cosmas and Damian. This icon is of the holy martyrs and un-mercenary saints from Asia, who have no date given, but are commemorated on November 1. They are holding jars of medicine and are looking up to Immanuel blessing from the clouds above.

90. The Holy Orthodox Princes Boris and Gleb
Св. Благовѣр. Князья Борисъ и Глѣбъ
Стый мⷱникⷮ кна́зⷯ боріⷭⷯ | стый мⷱникⷮ кна́зⷯ глѣбⷯ
The Slavonic inscription says а҃гглⷯ г҃ⷣенⷩ ѿ престола бꙋжꙋ́ сов́ѣцⷪⷮⷮⷮ почⷭⷮти тверⷪⷠⷤ "The Angel of the Lord from the Divine Throne announcing the difficult honor." These two sons of St. Vladimir refused to fight their brothers for the throne after their Father's death. They accepted death calmly and are called "Passion-bearers," the first saints glorified in Rus. The saints are commemorated on July 24.

---

[9] *Great Collection of Lives of the Saints*, Vol. II, page 393.

91. Monastic St. Anthony the Roman
Св. Препод. Антоній Рымлянинъ
Преп а҆нто́нїй рымла́нинх

St. Anthony was in born in Rome of Orthodox parents in 1067. At the age of nineteen he gave his possessions to the poor and went to pray on a rock on the sea shore. One day a piece of this rock took the Saint across the seas and rivers. Three days later he arrived in Novgorod in 1106 not speaking a single word of Russian. Our sketch shows him standing on a stone in a river praying for his monastery before the Mother of God and the Christ Child. He died on August 3, 1147 and is commemorated on January 17.

92. The Monastic Saint Alexander of Svir
Св. Преп. Александръ Свирскій
Ст҃ый прпⷣбный а҆леѯа́ндрх свирскїй

St. Alexander is celebrated on August 30. He is praying for his monastery to the ст҃а́а тро́нца Holy Trinity. His scroll says, "Do not worry about me, brothers, it is for this reason I ..." The oval at the bottom says, "This monastic father, St. Alexander, was born in the region of White Lake of a landowning father whose son became a monastic in the Cyrilov Monastery and died in the year 1553."

93. Monastic St. Nilus of Stolbensk
Св. Преп. Нилъ Столбенскій
Преподобный нилх столбенскїй

This saint lived on grass and acorns. He went to live on the Stolbensk Island where truly vicious people tried to kill him by setting the forest on fire. He died in 1554 while standing on crutches on which he rested instead of sleeping on a bed. Our sketch shows the Saint praying to Christ for his monastery on an island. The Saint in repose is lying in front of an icon of Immanuel. St. Nilus is celebrated on December 7.

94. St. Procopius of Ustyuzh Miracle Worker
Св. Прокопій Устюжскій Чуд.
Ѻ҆бразх ст҃а́гѡ проко́пїа о҆у҆стюжскагѡ чꙋдотво́рца

The holy righteous Procopius was a German from the city of Lubeck. He came with some German businessmen to Novgorod and accepted Orthodoxy in the Khutinsky Monastery. He eventually became a "fool for Christ" and died in 1303. The written description says that he is middle aged with a beard like St. Cosmas, has a purple cloak coming down from his left shoulder, and in his hand are three crutches. He has boots on his feet, but his knees are bare.[10] He is commemorated on July 8.

95. The Appearance of the Mother of God to George and Selected Saints
Явленіе Б. М. Георгію и Избранные Святіе

Ꙗвлѣнїе прест҃ыѧ бц҃ы ꙗ́же ꙗвлѣнїе | Ст҃ый мїхаи́лꙁ а̑рхаг҃гла, ст҃ый і̑ѡа́ннꙁ, ст҃ый васі́лїй, ст҃ый а̑нтѵ́па

The top inscription divided by the Holy Mandylion says, "The Appearance of the most holy Theotokos which appearance | Archistrategos Michael, St. John, St. Basil, St. Antipas. From left to right we see the "Appearance of the Theotokos to George" (See Sketch 2:51), St. Michael the Archangel, St. John the Forerunner, St. Basil the Great, Hieromartyr Antipas, bishop of Pergamus, mentioned in Revelation 2:13. St. Antipas is celebrated on April 11. Bottom row: St. Tykhon of Amathus, Holy Righteous Anna, Great Martyr Nikita, Great Martyr Andrew Stratelates, Holy Martyr Leontius, Monastic St. Michael of Maleina, Monastic St. Daniel Stylite, Blessed Basil of Moscow, and Monastic St. Matrona.

96. "Week" or "Six Days"
Недѣля или Шестодневъ

The Slavonic inscriptions have not been preserved in this drawing. The Russian title literally means "no work" or "Sunday" or a "week." Our week icon has icons of "The Resurrection" for Sunday, "The Synaxis of Bodiless Hosts" for Monday, "The Synaxis of St. John the Forerunner" for Tuesday, "The Annunciation" for Wednesday, "The Washing of the Apostles' Feet" ѹ̑мовѣнїе нѡ́гꙁ for Thursday, "The Crucifixion" for Friday, and "All Saints" for Saturday. The other Slavonic inscriptions are found elsewhere in these volumes. Each icon represents the person or event given special veneration on each day of the week.

---

[10] *An Icon Painter's Notebook*, page 177.

MATERIALS FOR THE HISTORY OF RUSSIAN ICONOGRAPHY

1. **Fatherhood**
   Отечество
   Ѻ҆те́чество

In the tradition of the Russian Church before an icon can be venerated it has to be blessed. In the "Book of Needs"[11] we find "The Order for the Blessing and Consecration of Icons of the most holy life-giving Trinity in the Likeness of the Three Angels, or the Baptism or the Transfiguration or the Descent of the Holy Spirit." Thus, according to the church service books we have four different icons of the Holy Trinity, but no service to bless the icon of "The Fatherhood." All other representations of the Holy Trinity have been forbidden expressly in both the Greek and Russian Churches. This sketch is essentially the same icon as "Fatherhood" Vol. I, Sketch 1:18. The standard of Orthodoxy is whether something conforms to the teaching of the ecumenical and local councils and the holy fathers. Miracles, local aberrations and individual opinions do not determine whether something is Orthodox. See the Appendix for some decrees regarding icons.

2. **Fatherhood**
   We have another similar *Paternitas* icon with the four evangelists represented on the sides.

3. **Fatherhood**
   This variation, also called the "Western Type," shows the most holy Mother of God and St. John the Forerunner, similar to the "Sophia - The Divine Wisdom" icon.

4. **The Savior**
   Спаситель
   І҆и҃с х҃с гд҃ь вседержи́тель

This is the first of six variations of the "Lord Almighty" showing only the Lord's head. The double line outlining the hair and garments indicates a gold line. The icon probably had a dark background.

---

[11] Тре́бникъ [Part 2, Synodal Typographia, Moscow 1906,] page 105. [In Church Slavonic.]

5. The Savior

This is a very fine drawing with the complete inscriptions. Notice the Lord's eye is the center point of the halo.

6. The Savior

There is something lacking in this tracing. It is similar to the famous head of Christ by St. Andrew Rublev surviving from the Deisis of Zvenigorod, but lacks the grace and serenity of that famous icon.

7. The Savior

This is an example of the "Angry Eye" type of portrait of our Lord. Instead of staring at us, the Lord seems to be looking over our heads.

8. The Savior

This sketch shows the Lord in a very reflective and serene mood. Although some people say that "icons always look sad," this is the only one that struck me as "sad."

9. The Savior

Here the Lord Jesus Christ has a very oval shaped face with the extra folds of his cloak associated with a bust portrait.

10. The Savior of the "Wet Beard"
Спасъ Мокрая Борода
Ѡбразъ гда бга и спа ншгw ійса хрта

The inscription should be "Image of our Lord, God and Savior Jesus Christ" written out under the Holy Face with їс хс written a second time. The original icons very often were large icons on the iconostasis measuring 53 by 46 inches as in the Dormition Cathedral in the Moscow Kremlin.

11. The Savior of the "Wet Beard"

The "Wet Beard" icons are among the most ancient depictions of the Lord and date from early Christian times. This sketch shows the placing of the Lord's name.

12. The Image of the Lord "Not Made by Hands"
Нерукотворений Образъ Господень
Стый нерукотворенїн ѡбразъ гда ншгw іса ха

This is a very simple "Mandylion" icon. The original icon measures 10½ by 13 inches. It has the lettering оубрусъ the Slavonic translation of σουδάριον "handkerchief." The cloth is decorated with gold figures. The icon dates from the end of the seventeenth century found in the Ascension Women's Monastery.[12]

13. The Lord Immanuel
Господь Еммануилъ
Ї҃с х҃с г҃дь є҆мманꙋилх
See Sketches 1:13 and 14.

14. The Lord Immanuel
The blackness indicates "light." The original probably had a very dark background. The lettering is gold and the Christ Child had abundant gold lines on His garments.

15. "You are a Priest Forever According to the Order of Melchizedek"
Ты Еси Їерей во Вѣкъ по чину Мелхиседекову
Ты̀ є҆сѝ і҆ере́й во вѣ́кх по чинꙋ̀ мелхїседе́ковꙋ
The title is taken from Hebrews chapter 5:6, a quote from Psalm 110:4. The image is very confusing showing the "Western Type" Trinity at the top. Then again the Holy Trinity on the Cross: "The Ancient of Days," the Holy Spirit as a young man and the Lord Jesus Christ as a crucified seraph. There is the eight-pointed star of the "Eternal Eighth Day," the symbols of the evangelists, and two women's heads representing perhaps the sun and the moon. This is an example of the fantasy icons forbidden by the Orthodox Church.

16. "The Unsleeping Eye" of our Lord Jesus Christ
Недреманное Око Господа нашего Iисуса Христа
Недрема́нное о҆́ко г҃да на́шегѡ і҆и҃са х҃рта̀
We see the Lord Jesus Christ as a youth resting on a couch with the Mother of God and two angels of the Lord attending Him. This is an illustration of Psalm 120:4 "He who keeps you will not slumber. Behold, He who keeps Israel shall neither slumber nor sleep." (NKJ). The icon is more decorative than devotional.

17. The Mid-feast or the Twelve-year-old Jesus Christ in the Temple
Преполовеніе или 12ᵀᴹ Лѣтній IC ХС во Храмѣ
Преполовѣ́нї҆е г҃не
See the notes to Sketch 1:20. The Mother of God and St. Joseph are not represented here, but the central building reminds one of the rotunda of the Church of the Resurrection (Holy Sepulcher) in Jerusalem.

---

[12] Sketch 2:12 is missing from the copies of the original available. It is replaced with this drawing from Pokrovsky, page 87.

18.   The Transfiguration of the Lord
Преображеніе Господне
Преѡбраженїе гда ншгѡ Ійса хрта
See the notes to Sketch 1:21 Notice our Lord is touching St. John slightly left of center.

19.   The Transfiguration of the Lord
In this unique variation the apostles are viewing the actual Transfiguration contrary to traditional iconography. Again below the Savior is touching James and John on the shoulder. These variations distract the viewer from the importance of our Lord Jesus Christ. His Person was drawn significant smaller because of the introduction of confusing details. An individual's imagination has confused the teaching of the Gospel.

20.   The Entrance of the Lord into Jerusalem
Входъ во Іерусалимъ Господа
Вхо́дъ во іерꙋсали́мъ гда нш҃гѡ Ійса хрта̀
This is a typical and straightforward design for the Palm Sunday icon. Notice the rotunda of the Church of the Resurrection in Jerusalem.

21.   The Entrance of the Lord into Jerusalem
This variation draws the citizens of Jerusalem on a larger scale.

22.   Jesus Christ on Trial before Pilate
IC. XC. на Судѣ предъ Пилатомъ
Привод́енїе Ійса хрта въ пїлатꙋ
This is a fine illustration of an event in our Lord's Passion. There were sets of Passion icons which were venerated during Holy Week in Russia.

23.   The Crucifixion
Паспятіе Господне
Распа́тїе гда бга нш҃гѡ Ійса хрта̀
This sketch is very similar to Vol. I Sketch 1:74. The Mother of God and St. John the Theologian are alone before the Cross.

24.   The Crucifixion of the Lord
This is the standard design for the Crucifixion. The beams of the Cross are somewhat heavy and the perspective of the sides is extreme. It is not clear what the extra lines over Christ's arms signify and should be deleted.

25. The Crucifixion of the Lord

This is a very complete icon of the Crucifixion with the two thieves. Notice the Ancient of Days and the Holy Spirit as a dove above the Crucified. Although uncanonical and superfluous, they do not confuse or distract like Sketch 2:15. The angels are holding chalices to catch the most precious Blood of Christ and the walls of Jerusalem actually represent the city.

26. The Descent from the Cross

Снятіе со Креста Господа Нашего Іисуса Христа

Снѧ́тїе съ кр͠та̀ г͠да̀ б͠га нш͠гω і͠иса хр͠та̀

A ladder is leaning against the Cross. Нїкодимъ Nicodemus is holding Christ around the waist; the Mother of God is standing on a stool and holding His shoulders; St. John the Theologian is standing off to the left side and і͠осифъ Joseph of Arimathea is pulling out the nails. The holy myrrh-bearing women are lamenting the death of Christ.

27. The Descent from the Cross

This is a very elaborate and distracting variation of the theme. There are no inscriptions so the third man taking Christ's body down from the Cross is unidentified. On the left The Mother of God and St. John the Theologian are conversing while on the right the myrrh-bearing women are looking on. Notice the chalice next to the cross, the sign on top and the clouds in the upper corners.

28. Deisis

Деисисъ

This icon would not be inscribed "Deisis," but would have the usual inscriptions for our Lord, the Mother of God and St. John the Forerunner who is depicted with wings. Unlike "The Queen Stood," they are wearing their usual garments. The throne and footstool are very highly ornamented to signify the majesty of Jesus Christ.

29. Deisis

Деисисъ

С͠тый мїхаи́лъ а̑рха́гг͠лъ| і͠с х͠с | С͠тый гаврїи́лъ а̑рха́гг͠лъ

Our Lord Jesus Christ is on His throne in the center as the "Lord Almighty" holding His Gospel book open to а̑зъ е̑смь свѣ́тъ мі́рꙋ "I am the Light of the world..." (John 8:12) St. Michael the Archangel and St. Gabriel the Archangel are closest to His head and have their inscriptions written above. St. John the Forerunner is on the right holding a scroll saying, "Behold the Lamb of God... Repent!" as usual. The most holy Mother of God is on the left. The holy Apostles Peter and Paul are facing each other at the upper left and right.

30. Deisis or Week

Деисисъ или Седмица

This is a very elaborate deisis group and would have the usual inscriptions for each person in Slavonic. In the center are the Ancient of Days in the clouds and our Lord Jesus Christ on His throne. The following are the pairs of saints from the top down: the holy apostles Peter and Paul; archangels Michael and Gabriel; the Mother of God and St. John the Forerunner; monastic Ss. Sergius Radonezh and Barlaam of Chutin; monastic Ss. Zosimas and Sabbatius. St. George is behind the Mother of God and St. Demetrius is behind St. John the Forerunner. Ss. Basil the Great, Gregory the Theologian and John Chrysostom are behind St. Michael. Ss. John the Theologian, Alexis the Man of God, Constantine and Helen, Cosmas, Barbara and [monastic St. Anthony of the Pecherska Lavra] are behind St. Peter. Ss. Andrew the Apostle; Boris, Gleb and Vladimir; Damian, Catherine, Mary of Egypt and [monastic St. Theodosius of the Pecherska Lavra] are behind St. Paul. This icon was intended for personal use as an aid to devotion.

31. The Conception by St. Anna

Зачатіе Св. Анны

Зача́тїе ст҃ы́а а́нны, є҆гда̀ зача́тъ прест҃у́ю бц҃у.

Ст҃ы́й і҆ѡакі́мъ St. Joachim and ст҃а́а а́нна are embracing at the eastern gate of the Temple. At the top left we see а҃ г҃ an angel of the Lord speaking to St. Joachim and another angel speaking to Anna on the right. The Conception by St. Anna is celebrated on December 9 and the Synaxis of Ss. Joachim and Anna is on September 9.

32. The Nativity of the Mother of God

Рождество Б. М.

Рождество̀ прест҃ы́а влⷣчцы нш҃еа бц҃ы | и҆ приснѡдв҃ы мр҃і́н

The inscription on top is "The Nativity of our Lady the Theotokos." Below this on the left are "The prayer of St. Joachim in the desert" and on the right "The prayer of St. Anne in the garden." The upper tier of the icon has the Conception of St. Anna as above. "Angel of the Lord" is spelled out over each angel, but the center lettering is the end of the main inscription at the top. In the middle tier on the left we see the usual depiction of the Birth of the Mother of God. Three maids are waiting on St. Anna. Below we see the maids bathing the infant Mary. On the right we see Ss. Joachim and Anna holding and rejoicing over the birth of Mary. On the bottom is a fanciful depiction of birds drinking from a fountain.

33. The Nativity of the Mother of God

In this sketch the basic elements of the icon are rearranged. On the bottom right is a scene not present elsewhere. It appears St. Anna is presenting the Mother of God as a young child to St. Joachim.

34. The Annunciation of the Mother of God
Благовѣщеніе Б. М.
Блговѣщеніе прест҃ыѧ бц҃ы

The Archangel Gabriel announcing to the Virgin Mary that she would be the Mother of God. This is the basic design for an icon of the Annunciation celebrated on March 25.

35. The Annunciation of the Mother of God
We have a variation of the same.

36. The Annunciation of the Mother of God
The Mother of God is standing and Archangel Gabriel is walking. The Archangel in the other designs is in motion and very dynamic. A curious servant is peeking out from behind a column.

37. The Annunciation of the Mother of God
Here a servant is sitting before the Mother of God.

38. The Icon of the M. of G. "Blessed is the Womb" or "the Nursing Mother"
Икона Б. М. Блаженно Чрево или Млекопитательница
Образъ прест҃ыѧ бц҃ы блаженне чрево - млекопитательница

The original icon is in the old tower of St. Sabbas called *Typikareion* belonging to the Chilandar Monaster on Mount Athos. It was taken there by St. Sabbas, the Archbishop of Serbia, from St. Sabbas Lavra near Jerusalem to fulfill a prophesy by its founder. The icon shows the Christ Child nursing from under a fold of the Virgin's maphorion.

39. The "Bogolyubsky" Icon of the Mother of God
Боголюбская Икона Б. М.
Образъ прест҃ыѧ бц҃ы бголюбскїѧ

This is a variation of an icon that originally had no saints. The most holy Mother of God is facing the Savior in the clouds holding a scroll that might say, "O Master, Almighty Son and my God, lend Your ear. Hear the prayer of Your mother praying in Your holy name. Hear me, and have mercy on everyone who calls on your holy name." The Savior's scroll might say, "My ear is ready to hear your request, which anyone might ask in your name, My dear mother, who stands and prays for mercy for the human race." Kneeling before her in prayer is someone who looks like the prophet Daniel. Below him are the miracle working hierarchs of Moscow Alexis, Peter and Philip. Beneath them are two monastic saints, perhaps Sergius of Radonezh and Barlaam of Chutin. The "Bogolyubsky" icon is celebrated on June 18 and has many variations.

40. The Mother of God "Joy of All Who Sorrow"
Икона Б. М. Всѣхъ Скорбящихъ Радость
Ѻбразъ престыА бцы _ всѣхъ скорбАщихъ радость

This icon is celebrated on October 24 and has at least seventeen variations illustrating the good deeds which should be done by all Christians. See the notes to Vol. I, Sketch 1:11. At the top in the clouds is the "Fatherhood" group attended by two angels holding ceremonial fans, and the sun and the moon. In this icon the Mother of God is not holding a scepter, but is pointing out "The Way," namely Jesus Christ. Above the scrolls are four unidentified saints. The scrolls may contain the text of a popular liturgical hymn: "O Joy of all who suffer and Intercessor for those treated unjustly, Comfort for strangers, Haven of the storm-tossed, Healer of the infirm, Protection and Intercessor for the helpless, Staff for the aged: you are the most pure Mother of the Most High God: hasten, pray and save your servants!" The box under her feet may have the text: "You will tread on the asp and the basilisk, and you will trample the lion and the serpent." [Psalm 90:13]

41. The "Dnieper" Icon of the Mother of God
Днѣпрская Икона Б. М.
Ѻбразъ престыА бцы касперювскїА

See the notes to Sketch 1:39. The lettering underneath says, "A painting of Ivan Prokopiev student."

42. "Dnieper" Icon of the Mother of God
This is another variation of the same icon.

43. "The Dove" or Konevsky Icon of the Mother of God
Голубицая или Коневская Икона Б. М.
Ѻбразъ престыА бцы коневскїА

The Konev icon of the Mother of God was taken from Mount Athos to Russia by the monastic St. Arsenius of Konev in 1393. It was placed in the Men's Monastery in Konev on one of the islands in Ladoga Lake connected with the Monastery of Valamo. The icon takes its name from the dove the Christ Child is holding. Notice the string tied to the dove held in His other hand.

44. The "Passion" Icon of the Mother of God
Страстная Икона Б. М.
Ѻбразъ престыА бцы страстнїА

See the notes in Vol. I, Sketch 1:8. This is a "mirror image" of the usual design. The Virgin's robe is very ornate and the Christ Child's robes are very bright indicated by the almost black drawing.

45.   **The "Passion" Icon of the Mother of God**

This variation is so removed from the original by Andreas Ricco that comparing them, one would not know they were the same icon. Above the angels is the heavenly firmament adorned with the sun, stars and the moon. The angels are holding respectively the Cross and the spear and reed. The Christ Child is holding His cheek against the Virgin's cheek.

46.   **The "Tykhvin" Icon of the Mother of God**
Тихвинхкая Икона Б. М.
Ѻбразъ прест҃ыѧ бц҃ы тѵхвннскїѧ

See the note in Vol. 1 to Sketch 1:36. The lettering underneath says, "A Painting by Procopius Chirin."

47.   **The "Sweet Sorrow" Icon of the Mother of God**
Икона Б. М. Умиленіе
Ѻбразъ прест҃ыѧ бц҃ы оумиленїѧ

There are many icons of the Mother of God with the title "Sweet Sorrow." The name suggests the tender feeling in the representation rather than a type. This sketch is similar to the "Yaroslavl" icon.

48.   **The "Sweet Sorrow" Icon of the Mother of God**

This is another variation of a "Sweet Sorrow" icon.

49.   **The "Theodore" Icon of the Mother of God**
Ѳеодоробская Икона Б. М.
Ѻбразъ прест҃ыѧ бц҃ы ѳ҇еодѡрѡвскїѧ

The original is believed to be one of the icons painted by St. Luke the Evangelist. The extensive black areas are highlights.

50.   **The Miracle of the Icon "The Sign of the Mother of God"**
Чудо отъ Иконы Знаменія Б. М.
Чꙋдо ѿ їкѡны знаменїѧ бц҃ы

See the notes to Sketch 2:89 in Vol. I. In this sketch the artist represented the events on two tiers instead of three. On top we see Archbishop John coming out of the Church of the Savior holding a pole with the icon of "The Sign" and carrying it over the Volkhov Bridge. The people venerate the miraculous icon before it is taken to the kremlin which the Suzhdalians are besieging. The attack by the Suzhdalians is shown in the lower level. They are shooting arrows at the icon, which is set up on the wall, but the Virgin turns away from the Suzhdalians shedding tears. The Novgorodians are seen at the bottom advancing the attack to avenge the affront to the Virgin. In doing so, they are supported by heaven. We see Ss. Boris and Gleb riding at the head of the army.[13] The word over St. John says, "Master." The word on the bridge says, "bridge," over the water "Volkhov," the squiggle on the center right, "New Town." Over the saints' heads are written "Boris," "Gleb" and "John." The handwriting at the bottom says, "The holy miracle which occurred to save the new town [the literal meaning of the name "Novgorod"]. This drawing is by Alexis Jacob of the Sign of the Virgin."

51. The Appearance of the Mother of God to George
Явленіе Б. М. Георгію
Ка́кѡ га́вса преста́а бц҃а на бесѣ́да

Like the preceding icon, this icon is of historical interest. "How the Most Holy Theotokos Appeared in a Conversation" is the title at the top. At the top center we see the "Tykhvin" Icon. On the left a man in a little boat sees angels carrying the icon through the air. Below this we see the Mother of God sitting [on a log.] Opposite her is St. Nicholas the miracle worker to whom a church was dedicated at that place. They are speaking to Yurish, a nickname for George. She told him to put a wooden cross on top of the church. Yurish is speaking to the clergy below; above he appears to be falling from the tower.

52. St. Michael the Archangel
Св. Михаилъ Архангелъ
Ст҃ый мїхаи́лх архагг҃лх

Compare this icon to Sketch 1:56. St. Michael is wearing rich deacons' vestments; the orarion and hems are embroidered with seraphim. He has a staff in his right hand and a disk depicting the Synaxis of Angels with the Ancient of Days in his left hand. On the left the same angels are spearing a demon falling into the abyss. In the right-hand corner is the Miracle of Colossae with the monastic St. Archippus.

53. Michael the Archangel
Михаилъ Архангелъ
а҃ггл҃х храни́тель

The Lord Immanuel is above in the clouds, otherwise this sketch is ambiguous. The Russian title says "Archangel Michael" but the inscription on the sketch says "Guardian Angel." We see an angel either protecting or trampling a sleeping nude young man. In his right hand the angel is holding a cross with the lance and reed marked IC XC NIKA, and "King of Glory." He is holding a sword in his left hand.

---

[13] Onasch, page 364.

54. Archangels Michael and Gabriel
Архангелъ Михаилъ и Гавріилъ
Ст҃ый мїхаилъ а҆рхаг҃лъ | ст҃ый гаврїилъ а҆рхаг҃лъ

This is a very simple version of the Synaxis icon.

55. The Synaxis of Michael the Archangel
Соборъ Архангела Михаила
Собо́рх а҆рхїстратига мїхаила

In the center Jesus Christ, the Lord Immanuel is represented on a disk held by Archangels Michael and Gabriel. They are surrounded by a host of angels and seraphim. The Synaxis of St. Michael is celebrated November 8.

56. Prophet Elias
Пророкъ Илія
Ст҃ый прⷪрокъ и҆лїа

The prophet is blessing with his right hand and in his left he is holding a scroll on which is written, "I was very zealous for the Lord God Almighty."

57. The Taking up of the Prophet Elias into Heaven
Взятіе Пророка Иліи на Небо
Ѽгненое восхожде́нїе пророка бж҃їа и҆лїн

The Slavonic inscription might say, "The Fiery Ascent of the Prophet of God Elias." Viewing the icon from the middle of the left side we see Elias in a cave being fed by the raven. Below an angel is speaking to Elias and preparing him for his arduous journey. At the bottom center Elias and Elisha are preparing to cross the Jordan River. At the top the prophet Elias is dropping his mantle to Elisha who is standing below with his arms spread out.

58. The Prophet Daniel in the Lions' Den
Пророкъ Даніилъ во Рвѣ со Львами
Ст҃ый проро́къ данїилъ

At the top the Ancient of Days is blessing and holding an orb representing the universe or world. To the left an angel of the Lord is carrying the prophet Habbakuk by his hair, who has a basket of bread and cooked food which he is bringing to Daniel according to *Bel and the Dragon* in the Septuagint. Daniel is blessing with his right hand and holding a book which might say, "I saw a great mountain from which came the rock which was hewn without being touched by human hands."

59. John the Forerunner

Іоаннъ Предтеча

Ст҃ый їѡа́ннꙁ пред́те́ча

This sketch could be used to design an icon for a deisis group. "Behold the Lamb of God!" or "Repent, the kingdom of Heaven is at hand!" might be written on his scroll.

60. The Synaxis of John the Forerunner

Соборъ Іоанна Предтеча

Собо́рꙁ їѡа́нна пред́те́чи й кре́сти́тела гд҃на

We see St. John baptizing some men in the Jordan River while the scribes and Pharisees are discussing this among themselves. Above the Ancient of Days is blessing in the clouds. The Synaxis of St. John is observed on January 7.

61. Simeon the God-bearer

Симеонъ Богопріимецъ

Ст҃ый сѷмеѡ́нꙁ бг҃опр́ій́мецꙁ

This icon is a detail from the icon of the Meeting of the Lord.

62. Apostles Peter and Paul

Апостоли Петръ и Павелъ

Ст҃ый а҆п́лꙁ па́велꙁ | Ст҃ый а҆п́лꙁ пе́трꙁ

These are from a deisis group of head and shoulder length portrait icons. St. Paul is on the left facing St. Peter on the right. Ss. Peter and Paul are celebrated on June 29.

63. St. John the Theologian

Іоаннъ Богословъ

Ст҃ый їѡа́ннꙁ бг҃осло́вꙁ

This is a fine portrait of St. John the Theologian.

64. St. John the Theologian

St. John is opening the Gospel to the words, "In the beginning..." The Holy Spirit дх҃ꙁ ст҃ый is depicted as an angel with an eight-pointed star in his halo whispering into John's ear. This should not be done. Other icons designate him "Angel of the Lord."

65. St. John the Theologian

These are two more examples of head and shoulder portraits.

66.   The Evangelist Luke Paints the Icon of the Mother of God

Евангелистъ Лука Пишетъ Икону Богоматери

ѻ҆ а҆гі́ѻсѫ а҆по́столѫ и҆ є҆ѵⷢ҇ггелі́стѫ и҆ ст҃ый лꙋка̀

The Slavonic inscription says "The Holy Apostle and Evangelist and Saint Luke." At the top an angel among clouds and stars is holding the Gospel book open to the words, "In as much as many... (Luke 1:1)" To the left the most holy Mother of God is sitting on a throne and holding the Christ Child on her lap. St. Luke is sitting at his desk painting an icon of the Virgin and Child. The writing on the scroll is illegible. It might say, "St. Luke painted the first icon of the Mother of God holding our Lord Jesus Christ as a child in her arms." Even if St. Luke did not know the Savior as a child, the icon is a testimony that the iconographic tradition comes down to us from the Apostles.

67.   St. Nicholas the Miracle Worker

The spiritual purpose of an icon is to reflect the divine grace in a saint. In this head and shoulders portrait of St. Nicholas we see the strength and serenity associated with this most revered of saints.

68.   St. Nicholas the Miracle Worker "Mozhaisky"

Св. Николай Чудотворецъ Можайскій

ст҃ый николай чꙋдотворецъ

There are a number of miracle working icons of St. Nicholas. One of these in Mozhaisk in the vicinity of Moscow received special veneration. There is an episode concerning the history of an icon of Saint Nicholas brought to Russia from Byzantium which was placed in Zaraz (later Mozhaisk). This episode was woven into the account of the destruction of the city of Ryatsan by the Tartars in 1237... Even though so many icons of St. Nicholas were placed in the market places in Russia, there were many statues of him as well. These statues portray St. Nicholas is holding a drawn sword in one hand and a church in the other. It is possible that these wooden statues resulted from western influence.[14] Our sketch shows the Saint standing in an ornate firmament adorned with clouds and stars between miniature representations of the most holy Mother of God and the Lord Jesus Christ. His cross patterned phelonion is richly decorated with a cross motif on the lining. The sword indicates St. Nicholas is resolved to protect the Church by force, if necessary. He spent time in jail for striking the heretic Arius at the First Ecumenical Council.

---

[14] Tschizewskij, pages 15 and 17.

69. **The Three Hierarchs: Ss. John Chrysostom, Basil the Great and Gregory the Theologian**

Три Святителя Василій Бел. Їоаннъ Злат. и Григорій Богос.

Ст҃ый григо́рїй бг҃осло́въ | ст҃ый васі́лїй вели́кїй | ст҃ый їѡа́ннъ златоу́стъ

This straightforward representation of the three Saints shows them wearing plain vestments. The omophoria should have crosses. St. Basil holding his omophorion so his priest's stole can be seen.

70. **St. John the Forerunner and Moscow Hierarchs**

Їоанна Предтеча и Московскіе Святители Алексѣй и Филиппъ

Miracle Workers of Moscow

Московскіе Чудотворцы

Ст҃ый але҄ѯїй митрополі́тъ | ст҃ый їѡа́ннъ предте́ча | ст҃ый фїлі́ппъ митрополі́тъ

On top we see the Holy Mandylion. St. Alexis the Metropolitan of Moscow on the left and St. Philip the Metropolitan of Moscow on the right are turning to St. John the Forerunner in the center.

71. **The Moscow Miracle Workers**

Московскіе Чудотворцы

Miracle Workers of Moscow

Московскіе Чудотворцы

Ст҃ый але҄ѯїй митрополі́тъ; ст҃ый пе́тръ митрополі́тъ;
ст҃ый їѡ́на митрополі́тъ; ст҃ый фїлі́ппъ митрополі́тъ

The Slavonic inscription should say, "St. Alexis, Metropolitan; St. Peter, Metropolitan; St. Jonah, Metropolitan; St. Philip, Metropolitan." These saints are celebrated together on October 5. Although St. Philip of Moscow died in 1569, his commemoration was combined with the first three saints in 1875, effectively dating the original icon to 1875 or later. On top our Lord is represented on the Holy Mandylion supported by two angels.

72. **St. Leontius Metropolitan of Rostov**

Св. Леонтій Ростовскій Чуд.

Ст҃ый лео́нтїй росто́вскїй чу́дотво́рецъ

Compare this sketch to 1:75. Here he is wearing a very ornate brocade saccos. The white material behind his back is his omophorion. He is standing in prayer before the Mother of God with the Christ Child on a throne in heaven.

73. **Martyr Anastasia**
Мучиница Анастасіа
Ст҃а́ѧ вєлнкомꙋ́чнца а҆наста́сіа

There are several saints named Anastasia. This one is celebrated on December 22 and died in the year 304. She is wearing a light blue tunic and a scarlet cloak with a scarf on her head. She is holding a cross and standing in prayer before the Mother of God surrounded by angels.

74. **St. George the Victorious**
Георгій Побѣдоносецъ
Ст҃ы́й вєлнкомꙋ́чнкъ геѡ́ргїй побѣ́доносєцъ

St. George is probably best known for being the dragon slayer, but this event is not recorded in his *Life* nor is it mentioned in the church service sung in his honor. We see the usual depiction of St. George slaying the dragon, but an angel is receiving the crown of martyrdom from the Lord and then again is about to place it on St. George's head.

75. **Demetrius of Thessalonica**
Дмитрій Солунскій
Ст҃ы́й днмн́трїй сєлꙋ́нскїй

St. Demetrius is standing on one foot while blessing with one hand and holding a shield in the other. The very small letters on his cloak, the stripe across his breastplate and on his leggings read "green" and the letters on his elbows read, "scarlet."

76. **Great Martyrs Demetrius and George**
Великомуч. Дмитрій и Георгій
Ст҃ы́й вєлнкомꙋ́чнкъ геѡ́ргїй побѣ́доносєцъ | Ст҃ы́й днмн́трїй сєлꙋ́нскїй

Actually the holy great martyr and victory bringer George is standing on the left side in a very elaborate landscape under the icon "The Sign of the Mother of God." He has curly hair, a breastplate, a scarlet cloak, in his left hand is a sword in its scabbard and a cross in his right hand. His helmet is behind his right shoulder and a shield with a lance with a banner is behind his left shoulder. He has purple leggings and ocher boots. On the right side St. Demetrius is wearing a green cloak. He has a cross in his right hand and a lance with a banner in his right. His shield and helmet are behind his shoulders like St. George's.

77. **Great Martyrs George and Demetrius**
Великомуч. Дмитрій и Георгій
Ст҃ы́й вєлнкомꙋ́чнкъ геѡ́ргїй побѣ́доносєцъ | Ст҃ы́й вєлнкомꙋ́чнкъ днмн́трїй сєлꙋ́нскїй

This is a simpler version of the previous icon. One can insert an icon of the Savior above them.

41

78. Archdeacon Stephan and Martyr Catherine

Архидіаконъ Стефанъ и Великомуч. Екатерина

С҃тый стефанъ а҆рхїдїа́конъ | ст҃а́а вели́комч҃ца є҆катери́на

Dressed in deacons' vestments, St. Stephen is holding a money box. He is commemorated on December 27. St. Catherine is celebrated on November 24.

79. Martyrs Kirrik and Julitta

Муч. Кирикъ и Улита

С҃тый мч҃нкъ кїру́къ | ст҃а́а мч҃нца і҆у́ли́тта

These holy martyrs suffered in the year 305. St. Julitta is holding a scroll which says, "I thank you, O Lord, for having called my son first, and for making him worthy to suffer for the sake of Your holy name."

80. Seven Youths of Ephesus

Семь Отроковъ Ефескихъ

С҃тїи о҆́троцы спа́щихъ, и҆́же во є҆фе́сѣ

The title below Christ Immanuel says, "The holy sleeping youths in Ephesus" The three saints at the top from left to right are і҆амвлі́хъ Jamblicius, Маѯїмїлїа́нъ Maximilian and Дїонѵ́сїй Dionysius. The four saints beneath are Мартїнїа́нъ Martinian, Кѡнстанті́нъ Constantine, А҆нтѡ́нїй Anthony and і҆ѡа́ннъ John. Their feast days are October 22 and August 4.

81. The Nine Holy Martyrs in Cyzicus

Девять Мучениковъ иже въ Кизицѣ

О҆́бразъ ст҃ы́хъ деѧти́ мч҃нкъ и҆́же въ кѷзі́цѣ

At the top center Jesus Christ has nine crowns prepared for His holy martyrs. Clockwise from the Savior are eleven lozenges corresponding to the saints in the central field: "Christ God crowned the sufferers by giving them grace to remove suffering from the people." "С҃тый ѳеогні́дъ St. Theognes, beaten with leather straps with iron nails and cleats, departed first. а҃ 1" "С҃тый ру́фъ St. Rufus was beaten with iron teeth, burned limbs and suffered martyrdom after many lashes. в҃ 2" "А҆нтїпа́теръ Antipater was beaten fiercely until his flesh fell off." "С҃тый ѳаѵма́сїй St. Thaumasius was killed by a spear after he was weakened by harsh servitude." "С҃тый а҆рте́ма St. Artemas was tied to a wheel and repeatedly rolled down a hill into a valley." "С҃тый фїлимѡ́нъ St. Philimon was torn apart with a hook over a long period of time." "С҃тый ѳеости́хъ St. Theostichus was scraped and burned with thorns." "С҃тый ѳеодо́тъ St. Theodotus was burned on a gridiron and finally was given over to suffer in terrible heat. є҃ 5" "С҃тый ма́гнъ St. Magnus was stretched out on a column, tormented with tongs and his limbs were cut off. д҃ 4" "To honor the crowns of the Nine Martyrs relieves fevers and malignant carbuncles." The martyrs are holding the instruments of their tortures. These nine martyrs are commemorated on April 29.

82. Martyr Nikita
Муч. Никита
Ст҃ый мч҃нкъ нїкита

The Saint is siting on a throne and beating a demon with a strange object while a jailer looks on. St. Nikita is celebrated on September 15.

83. Martyrs Cosmas and Damian
Муч. Козьма и Даміанъ
Ст҃ый мч҃нкъ козма и дамїанъ

There are two pairs of saints named Cosmas and Damian. This icon is another of the saints from Asia commemorated on November 1. See Sketch 1:89. They are holding jars of medicine and are looking up.

84. Ss. George, Cosmas, Damian, and Christopher
Муч. Георгій Козьма Даміанъ и Христофоръ
Ст҃ый великомч҃нкъ геѡргїй | Ст҃ый безсребник козма
Ст҃ый безсребнникъ дамїанъ | Ст҃ый мч҃нкъ хрїстофоръ

Ss. George, Cosmas and Damian are found elsewhere in these volumes. There is an article about Great-martyr Christopher in Volume I, page 17. The Appendix has a decree forbidding the saint to be depicted with a dog's head.

85. Martyrs Gurias, Samonas and Abibus
Муч. Гурій, Самонъ и Авивъ
Ст҃ый мч҃нкъ гȣрїй | ст҃ый мч҃нкъ самѡнъ | ст҃ый мч҃нкъ авівъ

These holy martyrs died in the year 306 and are celebrated on November 15.

86. Forty Martyrs at Sebaste
Сорокъ Мучениковъ Севастійскихъ
Ст҃їи м̄ мч҃нцы въ е҃зерѣ

These holy martyrs are celebrated on March 9 and are found elsewhere in these volumes.

87. Forty Martyrs at Sebaste
On the bottom we have the usual design for the icon. This sketch illustrates that the Holy Martyrs have chosen to serve the Heavenly King rather than an earthly king. The guard who is taking the place of the faint-hearted soldier in the bathhouse sees the crowns prepared above. Our Lord dressed as a Byzantine emperor on a throne is assisted by angels who are about to distribute the crowns.

88.   Martyr Andrew Stratelates and Mary of Egypt
Муч. Андрей Стратилатъ и Марія Египетская

Ст҃ый мч҃нкъ андрей стратилатъ | мр ҂д҃ | Преподобнаѧ маріа єгѷптскаѧ

The Icon of the Mother of God "Of the Don" is at the top of an elaborate landscape. (See Vol. I Sketch 2:15.) St. Andrew Stratelates (August 19) is looking toward the Icon while holding his lance and shield. His helmet is on his shoulder. Monastic St. Mary (April 1) is opposite in an attitude of prayer.

89.   Princes Boris and Gleb
Князья Борисъ и Глѣбъ

Ст҃ый мч҃нкъ кнѧзъ борисъ | ст҃ый мч҃нкъ кнѧзъ глѣбъ

The Saints are standing before the Heavenly King. They have removed their earthly crowns in order to receive their heavenly crowns. The Gospel book might be opened to "Whoever will confess Me before men, him will I confess also. Matthew 10:32" (See the notes to Sketch 1:90.)

90.   Princes Boris and Gleb
The Princes are standing before the "Image not made by Human Hands." After baptism the brothers were known as Roman and David.

91.   Princes Boris and Gleb and Vladimir
Князья Борисъ Глѣбъ и Владиміръ

Ст҃ый кнѧзъ борисъ | Ст҃ый кнѧзъ владиміръ | Ст҃ый кнѧзъ глѣбъ

St. Vladimir, known as Basil after baptism, is honored on July 15; Ss. Boris and Gleb on July 24.

92.   From the Life of Boris and Gleb "Passers-by Hear the Singing of Angels"
Изъ Житія Бориса и Глѣба. Слышаша Мимоходящіе Ангелское Пѣніе

After the death of St. Vladimir in 1015, there was a struggle for the throne among his sons. The oldest, Svyatopolk, seized power and began planning the elimination of his brothers Boris, Gleb and Yaroslav. They refused to fight against their brother to avoid further bloodshed and decided to await their fate passively, following the example of Jesus Christ. For this reason they are called martyrs. According to St. Nestor's account, Boris was attacked after saying his evening prayers while laying on his couch. While still alive he was loaded on a wagon and stabbed through the heart. Afterwards his body was carried secretly to Vyshegorod where it was buried in the church of St. Basil. Gleb was stabbed on his boat by his own cook and his body was thrown on the shore between two tree trunks, but afterward they took him away to bury him beside his brother.[15] Our icon is a very fanciful depiction of St. Nestor's account. To the right of top center we see a servant telling St. Gleb about his brother Boris' murder. Below St. Gleb's body is lying between the two tree trunks near the river. A light shines down from the heavenly sphere and two angels are standing in an attitude of wonder. On the right two shepherds are speaking to each other.

93. St. Alexis the Man of God
Алексѣй Человѣкъ Божій
Стый алеξій человѣкъ бжїй

St. Alexis (March 17) is standing in the desert with his arms crossed.

94. Ss. Alexis the Man of God

St. Alexis is standing in prayer before an icon that has not been reproduced in our sketch. The city of Rome is behind him. Sketch 93 a was placed on this page to show a variation in the arms.

95. Mary of Egypt and Alexis the Man of God
Марія Египетская и Алексѣй Человѣкъ Божій
Пρεποдόбнаа маρία ἐгυπετϲκαα | Стый алеξій человѣкъ бжїй

The two Saints are standing together in prayer before the Holy Mandylion.

96. Mary of Egypt
Марія Египетская
Пρεποдόбнаа маρία ἐгυπετϲκαα

Here the Saint is standing in prayer before an icon that has not been reproduced here.

97. Blessed Basil
Василій Блаженный
ὁ ἅгїοϲъ валίлїй блажέнный

The holy righteous blessed Basil, fool for the sake of Christ, miracle worker of Moscow, was not afraid of anyone. After Liturgy one day he said to Tsar Ivan the Terrible, "I saw that you were not in church today, but somewhere else." The Tsar replied, "I was nowhere else except in church." "Your words are not true, O Tsar. I saw you mentally strolling on the Sparrow Hills building a palace." The Saint is depicted without clothes standing in prayer before the Savior in the heavenly sphere. St. Basil died on August 2, 1552 and was buried in St. Basil's Chapel of the Protection Cathedral on the Red Square in Moscow.

---

[15] Zenkovsky, page 87.

98. Monastic Saint Nikita Pereyaslavsky
Никита Перьяславскій
Преподо́бный нїкн́та пере́аславскїй

With the blessing of his spiritual father the Saint took upon himself the ascetic endeavor of a stylite. He locked himself in his cell. He put a small "column" in his room and never left it. He is holding a scroll on which is written, "Behold, I gave up all for Christ and fleeing, I hid myself in the wilderness waiting for God to save me from a weak spirit and turmoil." The Saint entered the heavenly kingdom on May 24, 1186.

99. Monastic Saint Sergius of Radonezh
Преподобный Сергій Радонежскій
Препѣбный се́ргїй ра́донежскїй

St. Sergius of Radonezh is among the most venerated of Russian saints. He is the founder of the Holy Trinity Monastery in Sergeiev Posad near Moscow. Here he is blessing and holding a scroll which says, "Pay close attention to yourselves, brothers, for the fear of God!" He died on September 25, 1392 and his relics were uncovered on July 5, 1422.

100. Creation of the World
Сотвореніе Міра
Вх нача́лѣ сотворѝ бгх нѐбо й зе́млю.

"In the beginning God created the heaven and the earth...(Genesis 1:1 and following)" would be the most appropriate title for this complex icon. If a person really believes Genesis 1:1, he will not find it difficult to believe anything else in the Bible. If God really created all things, then He controls all things and can do all things. The inscriptions have not been preserved in our sketch, but one would expect appropriate verses from Genesis were on the original. This icon does not follow Genesis very closely. At the top is the "Fatherhood." At the top left Jesus Christ is absent: there are an empty throne, the Holy Spirit and the "Ancient of Days." To the right under the firmament with the sun and moon the "Ancient of Days" wearing apostle garments is creating the heaven and the earth. Next He is dividing the water from the land. Next He is observing angels in the heavenly sphere driving demons into the jaws of hades. (This conflicts with the consensus of the holy fathers that Lucifer was cast out of heaven before the days of creation.) The "Ancient of Days" is silent; His arm is not raised. Under the first circle He is creating the animals; under this someone else in a tunic is speaking to lions and horses. On the right under the "jaws of hades" the "Ancient of Days" is creating Adam. In the center He is resting on a couch with the Holy Spirit above. To the left He is holding Jesus Christ crucified in a lozenge with the sun or moon. On the right He is with the "Crucified Seraph." These three fields are surrounded by a multitude of angels over the firmament with the sun and moon. In the lower left-hand corner the "Ancient of Days" is creating

Eve from Adam lying beside him. Next He and Adam are conversing. Then Adam and Eve are conversing with each other. In the center an angel is driving Adam and Eve out of Paradise. Next Adam and Eve are lamenting their loss of Paradise. Surrounded by angels blowing trumpets, an angel is speaking with an unidentified young man in a tunic. Below this, with a demon whispering into his ear, Cain in a short tunic is killing Abel in a fur tunic. Near the bottom center Adam and Eve are lamenting the loss of their son Abel. The book of Genesis should be bound together with the New Testament like the Psalter is. Our understanding of the Gospel presumes our understanding of how God revealed Himself in the Old Testament. Many pictorial elements in this icon have been forbidden repeatedly by the Church over the centuries. (See the Appendix.) This icon does not illustrate Genesis as well as a child's book can, but rather it introduces a clutter of elements foreign to Orthodoxy.

101. Twenty-first Chapter of the Apocalypse
21ая Глава Апокалыпсиса
Любовъ

St. John the Theologian was shown the spiritual beauty and the grandeur of the New Jerusalem; that is, the kingdom of Christ, which is to be revealed in all its glory in the Second Coming of Christ, after the victory over the devil. The image of this "new Jerusalem" represents the triumphant Church of Christ, adorned as the Lord's Bride in the purity and virtues of the saints. The Bride of the Lamb, the Holy Church, appeared in the form of a splendid great city descending from heaven. A high wall surrounds the city as a sign that no unworthy person can enter it.[16] On our sketch "Love" or "Charity" is written to the right of an angel descending from the heavenly sphere. The angel is speaking to St. John the Theologian standing on the mountain, "Come, I will show you the bride, the Lamb's wife. (Rev. 21:9)" Carried by angels we see the holy Jerusalem is descending with the Lord Immanuel blessing. Within its walls we see the Mother of God with representative saints on the left St. John the forerunner, Moses, several apostles and two nuns on the right.

---

[16] Averky, page 209.

Patterns of Old Russian Iconography from the Collection of M. V. Tyulin

The Authors dedicate their work to

Professor Alfred Alexandrovich Parland

as a token of their deepest respect, esteem and devotion to him.

LIST OF SKETCHES

Sketch 1. The Old Testament Trinity

Sketch 2. The Old Testament Trinity

Sketch 3. The Savior

Sketch 4. The Lord Almighty

Sketch 5. The Lord Almighty

Sketch 6. The Lord Almighty

Sketch 7. The Lord Almighty

Sketch 8. The Lord Almighty

Sketch 9. The Lord Almighty

Sketch 10. The Savior

Sketch 11. The Lord Almighty

Sketch 12. The Savior of Smolensk

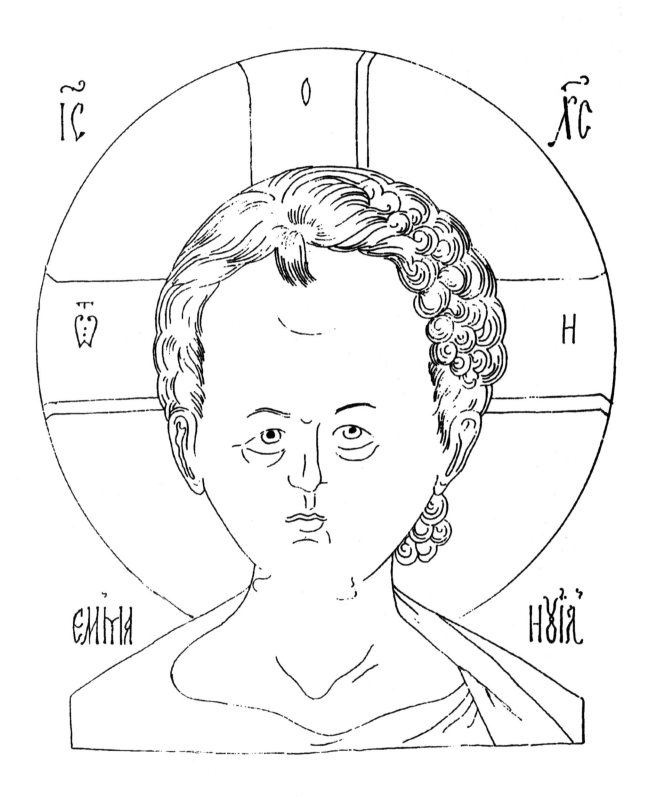

Sketch 13. The Lord Immanuel

Sketch 14. The Lord Immanuel

Sketch 15. The Great High Priest

Sketch 16. Image of the Lord "Not Made By Hands"

Sketch 17. The Nativity of Christ

Sketch 18. The Circumcision of the Lord and St. Basil the Great

Sketch 19. The Meeting of the Lord

Sketch 20. Mid-Pentecost

Sketch 21. The Transfiguration

Sketch 22. The Entrance of the Lord into Jerusalem

Sketch 23. The Eucharist

ПІЙТЕ ѾНЕА ВСИ ЄСТЬ КРОВЪ МОА ЄЖЕ ЗА ВЫ
ИЗЛИВАЕМОЕ ВОѠСТАВЛЕНИЕ ГРѢХОВЪ

IC ХC

Sketch 24. The Eucharist

Sketch 25. The Crucifixion of the Lord

Sketch 26. The Crucifixion

Sketch 27. Taking Our Lord Jesus Christ Down From the Cross

Sketch 28. The Resurrection of Christ

Sketch 29. The Only Begotten Son of God

Sketch 30 a. Deisis - The Theotokos

Sketch 30 b. Deisis - The Savior

Sketch 30 c. Deisis - St. John the Forerunner

Sketch 31 a. Deisis - St. Peter, St. Michael and the Theotokos

Sketch 31 b. Deisis - The Savior

Sketch 31 c. Deisis - Ss. John the Forerunner, Gabriel and Paul

Sketch 32. The King of Kings or The Queen Stood

Sketch 33. "Do Not Weep for Me, Mother"

Sketch 34. The "Akhremsky" Icon of the Mother of God

Sketch 35. The "Bogolyubsky" Icon of the Mother of God

Sketch 36. Icon of the Mother of God "The Child Leapt"

Sketch 37. Icon of the Mother of God "The Child Leapt"

Sketch 38. The "Georgian" Icon of the Mother of God

Sketch 39. The "Dnieper" Icon of the Mother of God

Sketch 40. Image of the Mother of God "The Sign"

Sketch 41. The "Iveron" Icon of the Mother of God

Sketch 42. Icon of the Mother of God "The Uncut Stone"

Sketch 43. The "Modensky" Icon of the Mother of God

Sketch 44. Icon of the Mother of God "Unexpected Joy"

Sketch 45. Icon of the Mother of God "O, All-hymed Mother"

Sketch 46. The "Petrov" Icon of the Mother of God

Sketch 47. The "Smolensk" Icon of the Mother of God

Sketch 48. The "Shuisko-Smolensk" Icon of the Mother of God

Sketch 49. The "Passion" Icon of the Mother of God

Sketch 50. Icon of the Mother of God "Of Three Joys"

Sketch 51. The Praises of the Most Holy Theotokos

Sketch 52. The Nativity of the Mother of God

Sketch 53. The Nativity of the Mother of God

Sketch 54. The Annunciation of the Mother of God

Sketch 55. The Dormition of the Mother of God

Sketch 56. St. Michael the Archangel

Sketch 57. The Guardian Angel

Sketch 58. The Guardian Angel

Sketch 59. St. John the Forerunner

Sketch 60. St. John the Forerunner

Sketch 61. St. John the Forerunner

Sketch 62. St. John the Forerunner

Sketch 63. The Decapitation of St. John the Forerunner

Sketch 64. The Decapitation of St. John the Forerunner

Sketch 65. The Synaxis of St. John the Forerunner

Sketch 66. Ss. John the Forerunner, John Chrysostom and the Martyr Nikita

Sketch 67. The Holy Forefather Jacob

Sketch 68. The Holy Prophet Elias

Sketch 69. St. Simeon the God-bearer

Sketch 70. The Holy Prophetess Anne

Sketch 71. St. John the Theologian

Sketch 72. St. John the Theologian

Sketch 73. The Holy Apostles Peter and Paul

Sketch 74. The Holy Apostles Peter and Paul

Sketch 75. St. Leontius of Rostov the Miracle Worker

Sketch 76. St. Nikita of Novgorod the Miracle Worker

Sketch 77. The Holy Metropolitan Jonah

Sketch 78. The Holy Metropolitan Alexis and Monastic St. Simeon

Sketch 79. The Three Hierarchs
Ss. Gregory the Theologian, Basil the Great and John Chrysostom

Sketch 80. The Three Hierarchs
Ss. Basil the Great, Gregory the Theologian, and John Chrysostom

Sketch 81. St. Nicholas the Miracle Worker

Sketch 82. St. Nicholas the Miracle Worker

Sketch 83. St. Nicholas the Miracle Worker

Sketch 84. Ss. Makarius, Nicholas, and Athanasius

Sketch 85. Ss. Demetrius, Nicholas, and Ignatius the God-bearer

Sketch 86. St. Demetrius of Thessalonica

Sketch 87. St. Demetrius of Thessalonica

Sketch 88. Holy Martyrs Gurias, Samonas and Abibus

Sketch 89. Holy Martyrs Cosmas and Damian

Sketch 90. The Holy Orthodox Princes Boris and Gleb

Sketch 91. Monastic Saint Anthony the Roman

Sketch 92. Monastic Saint Alexander of Svir

Sketch 93. Monastic Saint Nilus of Stolbensk

Sketch 94. Saint Procopius of Ustyuzh Miracle Worker

Sketch 95. The Appearance of the Mother of God to George and Selected Saints

Sketch 96. The Week or Six Days

Materials for the History of Russian Iconography

The Authors dedicate their work to the highly respected
Professor Nicholas Vasilievich Pokrovsky

LIST OF SKETCHES

Sketch 1. Fatherhood

Sketch 2. Fatherhood

Sketch 3. Fatherhood

Sketch 4. The Savior

Sketch 5. The Savior

Sketch 6. The Savior

Sketch 7. The Savior

Sketch 8. The Savior

Sketch 9. The Savior

Sketch 10. The Savior of the "Wet Beard"

Sketch 11. The Savior of the "Wet Beard"

Sketch 12. The Image of the Lord "Not Made By Hand"

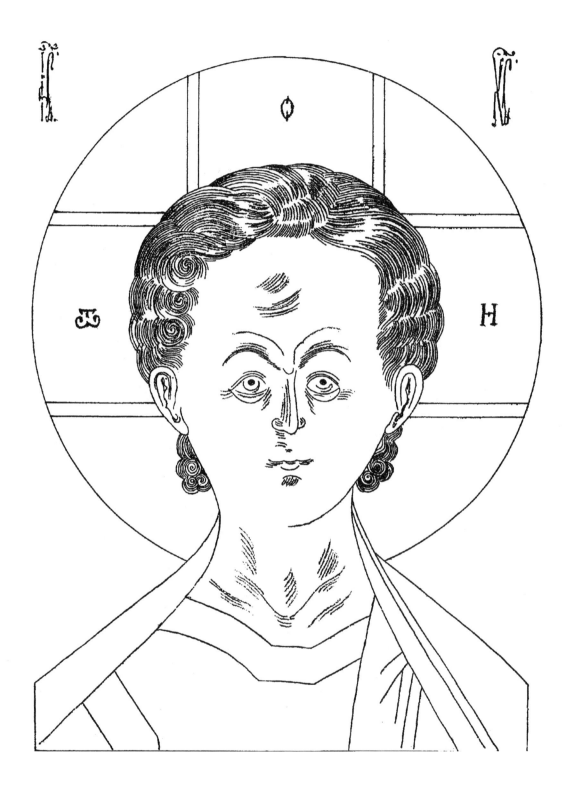

Sketch 13. The Lord Emmanuel

Sketch 14. The Lord Emmanuel

Sketch 15. "You are a Priest Forever According to the Order of Melchizedek"

Sketch 16. "The Unsleeping Eye" of our Lord Jesus Christ"

Sketch 17. Mid-feast or the Twelve-year-old Jesus Christ in the Temple

Sketch 18. The Transfiguration of the Lord

Sketch 19. The Transfiguration of the Lord

Sketch 20. The Entrance of the Lord into Jerusalem

Sketch 21. The Entrance of the Lord into Jerusalem

ПРИВѡДЕНІЕ ІС҃А ХР҃ТꙊ ВПИЛАТꙊ

Sketch 22. Jesus Christ on Trial before Pilate

Sketch 23. The Crucifixion of the Lord

Sketch 24. The Crucifixion of the Lord

Sketch 25. The Crucifixion of the Lord

Sketch 26. The Descent from the Cross

Sketch 27. The Descent from the Cross

Sketch 28. Deisis

Sketch 29. Deisis

Sketch 30. Deisis or Week

Sketch 31. The Conception by St. Anne

Sketch 32. The Birth of the Mother of God

Sketch 33. The Birth of the Mother of God

Sketch 34. The Annunciation of the Mother of God

Sketch 35. The Annunciation of the Mother of God

Sketch 36. The Annunciation of the Mother of God

Sketch 37. The Annunciation of the Mother of God

Sketch 38. The Icon of the Mother of God "Blessed is the Womb" or
"Virgin Suckling"

Sketch 39. The "Bogolyubsky" Icon of the Mother of God

Sketch 40. Icon of the Mother of God "Joy of All Who Sorrow"

Sketch 41. The "Dnieper" Icon of the Mother of God

Sketch 42. The "Dnieper" Icon of the Mother of God

Sketch 43. The "Dove" or "Konevsky" Icon of the Mother of God

Sketch 44. Icon of the Mother of God "Of the Passion"

Sketch 45. Icon of the Mother of God "Of the Passion"

Sketch 46. The "Tykhvin" Icon of the Mother of God

Sketch 47. Icon of the Mother of God "Sweet Sorrow"

Sketch 48. Icon of the Mother of God "Sweet Sorrow"

Sketch 49. The "Theodore" Icon of the Mother of God

Sketch 50. The Miracle from the Icon of the Mother of God "The Sign"

Sketch 51. The Appearance of the Mother of God to George

Sketch 52. St. Michael the Archangel

Sketch 53. St. Michael the Archangel

Sketch 54. Ss. Michael and Gabriel the Archangels

Sketch 55. The Synaxis of St. Michael the Archangel

Sketch 56. Prophet Elias

Sketch 57. Taking the Prophet Elias to Heaven

Sketch 58. Prophet Daniel in the Lion's Den

Sketch 59. St. John the Forerunner

Sketch 60. The Synaxis of St. John the Forerunner

Sketch 61. St. Simeon the God-bearer

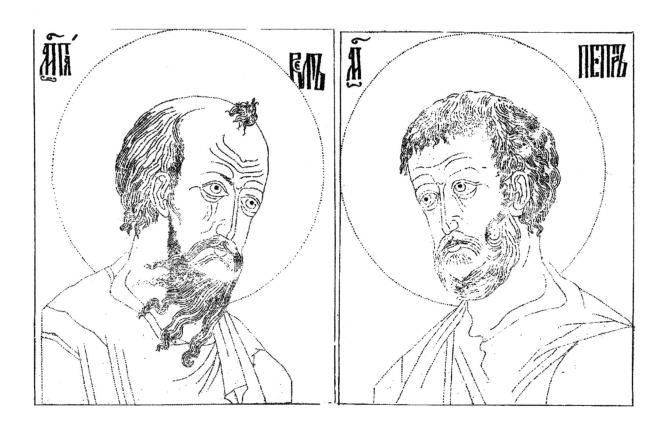

Sketch 62. Apostles Paul and Peter

Sketch 63. St. John the Theologian

Sketch 64 St. John the Theologian

Sketch 65. St. John the Theologian

Sketch 66. St. Luke Paints the Icon of the Mother of God

Sketch 67. St. Nicholas the Miracle Worker

Sketch 68. St. Nicholas the Miracle Worker "Mozhaisky"

Sketch 69. The Three Hierarchs
Ss. Basil the Great, Gregory the Theologian and John Chrysostom

Sketch 70. St. John with Ss. Alexis and Philip of Moscow

Sketch 71. The Miracle Workers of Moscow

Sketch 72. St. Leontius, Metropolitan of Rostov

Sketch 73. Holy Martyr Anastasia

Sketch 74. St. George the Victorious

Sketch 75. St. Demetrius of Thessalonica

Sketch 76. Great Martyrs Demetrius and George

Sketch 77. Great Martyrs George and Demetrius

с̃ стефанъ а̃рхидїа́конъ   с̃ великому̃ Єкатери́на

Sketch 78. Ss. Archdeacon Stephen and Great Martyr Catherine

Sketch 79. Martyrs Kirrik and Julitta

Sketch 80. The Seven Youths of Ephesus

Sketch 81. The Nine Martyrs at Cyzicus

Sketch 82. Martyr Nikita

Sketch 83. Martyrs Cosmas and Damian

Sketch 84. Martyrs George, Cosmas, Damian and Christopher

Sketch 85. Martyrs Gurias, Samonas and Abibus

Sketch 86. Forty Martyrs at Sebaste

Sketch 87. Forty Martyrs at Sebaste

Sketch 88. Martyr Andrew Stratelates and St. Mary of Egypt

Sketch 89. Princes Boris and Gleb

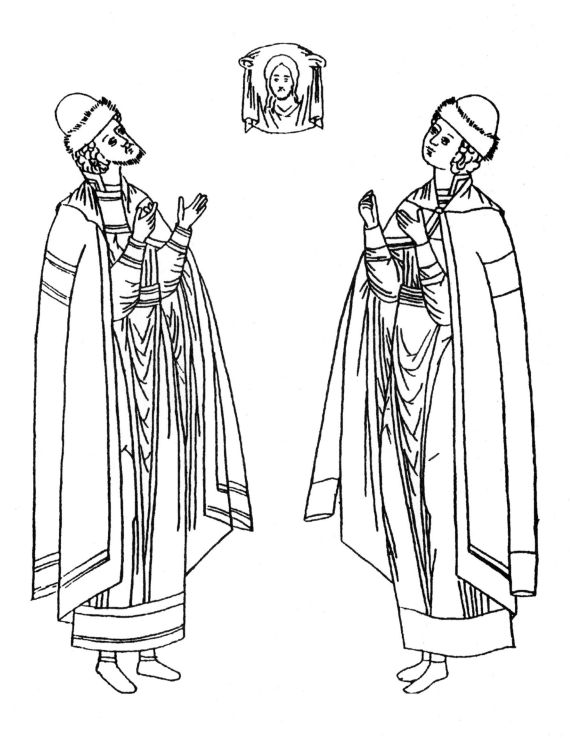

Sketch 90. Princes Boris and Gleb

Sketch 91. Princes Boris, Vladimir and Gleb

Sketch 92. From the Life of Boris and Gleb:
Passers-by Hear the Angelic Singing

Sketch 93 b. St. Alexis Man of God

Sketch 93 a

Sketch 94. St. Alexis the Man of God

Sketch 95. Ss. Mary of Egypt and Alexis the Man of God

Sketch 96. St. Mary of Egypt

Sketch 97. Blessed Basil

Sketch 98. St. Nikita Peryaslavsky

ВНИМА
ТЕСЕБѢ
БРАТНЕ
ПРЕЖДЕ
СТРАХВ
БЖИ ЇЙ

Sketch 99. Monastic Saint Sergius of Radonezh

Sketch 100. The Creation of the World

Sketch 101. The Twenty-first Chapter of the Apocalypse

APPENDIX

Father Steven Bigham has given iconographers a most useful work in his book "The Image of God the Father in Orthodox Theology and Iconography." Instead of quoting out of context and to avoid footnotes, it seemed better to reprint several important sections.

18. The Council of the Hundred Chapters (Stoglav), Moscow, 1551

Chapter 41, question 1:

On the icons of the Holy Trinity, some represent a cross in the nimbus of only the middle figure, others on all three. On ancient and on Greek icons, the words "Holy Trinity" are written on the top, but there is no cross in the nimbus of any of the three. At present, "IC XC" and "The Holy Trinity" are written next to the central figure. Consult the divine canons and tell us which practice one should follow.

The Reply: painters must paint icons according to the ancient models as the Greeks painted them, as Andrei Rublev and other renowned painters made them. The inscription should be "The Holy Trinity." Painters are in no way to use their imagination. [1]

23. The Great Council of Moscow, 1666-1667

Chapter 43: On the Iconographer and the Lord Sabaoth:

We decree that a skilled painter, who is also a good man (from the ranks of the clergy) be named monitor of the iconographers, their leader and supervisor. Let the ignorant not mock the ugly and badly painted holy icons of Christ, of His Mother, His saints. Let all vanity of pretended wisdom cease, which has allowed everyone habitually to paint the Lord Sabaoth in various representations according to his own fantasy, without an authentic reference ...

We decree that from now on the image of the Lord Sabaoth will no longer be painted according to senseless and unsuitable imaginings, for no one has ever seen the Lord Sabaoth (that is, God the Father) in the flesh. Only Christ was seen in the flesh, and in this way He is portrayed, that is, in the flesh and not according to His divinity. Likewise, the most holy Mother of God and other saints of God ...

To paint on icons the Lord Sabaoth (that is, the Father) with a white beard holding the only-begotten Son in His lap with a dove between them is altogether absurd and improper, for no one has ever seen the Father in His divinity. Indeed, the Father has

---

[1] Bigham, page 129.

A

no flesh, and it is not in the flesh that the Son was born of the Father before all ages. And if the Prophet David says, "from the womb, before the morning star, I have begotten you" [Ps 109/110: 31], such generation is certainly not corporeal, but unutterable and unimaginable. For Christ Himself says in the Holy Gospel, "No one knows the Father except the Son." In chapter 40, Isaiah asks: "What likeness will you find for God or what form to resemble His?" Likewise, the holy Apostle Paul says in chapter 17 of Acts: "Since we are God's offspring, we ought not to believe that the Godhead is the same as gold, silver, or stone shaped by human art and thought." St. John of Damascus likewise says: "Who can make an imitation of God the invisible, the incorporeal, the undescribable, and unimaginable? To make an image of the Divinity is the height of folly and impiety" [On the Heavens , Book IV, "On the Image"]. St. Gregory Dialogos forbade it in a similar way. This is why the Lord Sabaoth, who is the Godhead, and the engendering before all ages of the only-begotten Son of the Father must only be perceived through our mind. By no means is it proper to paint such images: it is impossible. And the Holy Spirit is not, in His nature, a dove: He is by nature God. And no one has ever seen God, as the holy evangelist points out. Nonetheless, the Holy Spirit appeared in the form of a dove at the holy baptism of Christ in the Jordan; and this is why it is proper to represent the Holy Spirit in the form of a dove, in this context only. Anywhere else, those who have good sense do not represent the Holy Spirit in the form of a dove, for on Mount Tabor He appeared in the form of a cloud, and in another way elsewhere. Besides, Sabaoth is not the name of the Father only, but of the Holy Trinity. According to Dionysius the Areopagite, Sabaoth is translated from the Hebrew as "Lord of Host." And the Lord of Hosts is the Trinity. And if the Prophet Daniel says that he has seen the Ancient of Days sitting on the throne of judgment, that is not taken to mean the Father, but the Son at His Second Coming, who will judge all the nations with His fearsome judgment.

Likewise, on icons of the Holy Annunciation, they paint the Lord Sabaoth breathing from His mouth, and that breath reaches the womb of the Most Holy Mother of God. But who has seen this, or which passage from Holy Scripture bears witness to it? Where is this taken from? Such a practice and others like it are clearly adopted and borrowed from people whose understanding is vain, or rather whose mind is deranged or absent. This is why we decree that henceforth such mistaken painting cease, for it comes from unsound knowledge. It is only in the Apocalypse of St. John that the Father [should be Son] can be painted with white hair, for lack of any other possibility, because of the visions contained in it.

It is good and proper to place a cross, that is, the Crucifixion of our Lord and Savior Jesus Christ, above the Deisis in the holy churches in place of Lord Sabaoth, according to the norm preserved since ancient times in all the holy churches of the eastern countries, in Kiev, and everywhere else except in the Muscovite State. This is a great mystery kept by the holy Church ...

B

We say this to shame the iconographers so that they stop making false and vain paintings, and from now on paint nothing according to their own ideas, without an authentic reference.[2]

26. Special Decrees of the Holy Synod of the Russian Church, 1722

April 6, 1722: On the antimensia ... , it is strictly forbidden to represent the Lord Sabaoth in the form of an old man, and the holy evangelists in the form of animals.

Ouspensky: ... the special ruling of the Holy Synod of the Russian Church in 1722 ... ordered that the image of God the Father on the antimensia be replaced by the inscription of the name of God in Hebrew, as a testimony to the divinity of Christ.

May 21, 1722:

Ouspensky: Aside from sculpture, the decree prohibited a whole series of icons "contrary to nature, to history, and to truth itself ... : the image of the Theotokos in labor during the Nativity of the Son, with a midwife next to her ... ; the image of Florus and Laurus with horses and grooms bearing fictional names," that is, traditional Orthodox subjects together with deviations. Thus, the martyr St. Christopher with the head of a dog; the Mother of God called "with three hands," no doubt with three natural hands instead of a pendant; the image of the burning bush; "the image of the Wisdom of God in the form of a young girl; the image of the creation of the world in six days by God, in which God is represented reclining on cushions ... ; the image of Lord Sabaoth in the form of an elderly man with his only Son on his lap and between them the Holy Spirit in the form of a dove," that is, the "Paternity"; the Annunciation with the Father blowing from His mouth, a crucified cherubim, and so forth.[3]

28. The Decree of the Holy Synod of Constantinople, 1776:

Concerning the image of two men side by side with a dove between them, the so-called New Testament Trinity:

It has been decreed by the Synod that the icon allegedly of the Trinity is an innovation. It is alien to the apostolic Orthodox Catholic Church and is not accepted by it. It infiltrated the Orthodox Church through the Latins.[4]

---

[2] Bingham, page 137.

[3] Bingham, page 144.

[4] Bingham, page 146.

BIBLIOGRAPHY

Averky, Archbishop of Jordanville. *The Apocalypse of St. John: An Orthodox Commentary*. Trans. and ed. by Fr. Seraphim Rose, Valaam Society of America, 1985.

Bingham, Fr. Steven. *The Image of God the Father in Orthodox Theology and Iconography and Other Studies*. Oakwood Publications, Torrance, CA 1995.

Dyachenko, Priest Magister Gregory. [*Complete Church Slavonic Dictionary*. Moscow, 1899] From Slavonic to Russian.

Great Collection of the Lives of the Saints, Trans. Fr. Thomas Marretta, Chrysostom Press, House Springs, MO 63051, 1995.

Kovalchuk, Archpriest Feodor S.,*Wonder-working Icons of the Theotokos*, translated and compiled from the Russian, Youngstown, Ohio, 1985.

Large Prayerbook, Holy Trinity Monastery, Printshop of St. Job of Pochaiev, 1964 [in Church Slavonic.]

Man of God: Saint John of Shanghai & San Francisco. Translated from the Russian, Compiled by Archpriest Peter Perekrestov, Nikodemos Orthodox Publication Society, Redding, California, 1994.

Melnick, Gregory. *An Icon Painter's Notebook: the Bolshakov Edition (An Anthology of Source Materials)* Oakwood Publications, 1995.

Onasch, Konrad. *Icons*. A. S. Barns and Company, New York, 1963.

[Pokrovsky, Professor N. V. 1809 - 1909 Ecclesiastical-Architectural Museum of the St. Petersburg Theological Academy 1879 - 1909.] In Russian.

[Poselyanin, E. ed. *Mother of God: a complete illustrated history of her earthly life and the miraculous icons sanctified by her name, St. Petersburg.*] No date, in Russian.

NKJ, The Holy Bible: The New King James Version. Thomas Nelson Publishers, Nashville, in many editions.

Orthodox Tradition. A quarterly published by the Center for Traditionalist Orthodox Studies, St. Gregory Palamas Monastery, P.O. Box 398, Etna, CA 96027.

The Tyulin Collection

The Psalter According to the Seventy. Holy Transfiguration Monastery, Boston, Massachusetts, 1974.

Skorobucha, Heinz. [*Mary: Russian Miraculous Images*] Verlag Aurel Bongers, Recklinghausen, 1967. [in German]

Stroganov Tradition: an Iconographer's Patternbook, trans. and ed. Fr. Christopher P. Kelley, Oakwood Publications, 1992.

Timchenko, S. V. *Russian Icons Today - Современная Православная Икона "Современник„* Moscow, 1994. [in both Russian and English]

Tschizewskij, Dmitrij. [*St. Nicholas,*] Verlag Aurel Bongers, Recklinghausen, 1975. [In German]

Zenkovsky, Serge A. *Medieval Russia's Epics, Chronicles, and Tales,* E. P. Dutton & Co., Inc., New York 1963.

E

INDEX

F

Glory to God for All Things!